Women Managers
in Human Services

Karen S. Haynes, Ph.D., Professor and Dean of the Graduate School of Social Work at the University of Houston, Houston, Texas, is the first and only female academic dean in the history of the University. She earned her Ph.D. in Social Work from the University of Texas at Austin School of Social Work and a Master's Degree in Social Work from McGill University in Montreal, Canada. Dean Haynes has held numerous local, state and national leadership positions in her professional career.

She is a Past-President of the National Alliance of Information and Referral Systems, currently serves on the Council of Social Work Education's Commission on Accreditation, was the state-wide chair of the Indiana Political Action Committee for Human Services and the Indiana Coalition for Human Services. She was Managing Director of International Resource Development in Cairo, Egypt. She co-edited *Accessing Human Services: International Perspectives* in 1984 with Dr. Risha Levinson and co-authored *Affecting Change: Social Workers in the Political Arena* with James S. Mickelson in 1986.

She is included in the first edition of *Two Thousand Notable American Women;* the ninth edition of *Who's Who in the World;* the first edition of *Who's Who Among Human Service Professionals* and the *International Directory of Distinguished Leadership*. She has presented numerous keynote speeches and conducted seminars and workshops nationally.

Women Managers in Human Services

Karen S. Haynes, Ph.D.

SPRINGER PUBLISHING COMPANY
New York

Copyright © 1989 by Springer Publishing Company, Inc.

Springer Publishing Company, Inc.
536 Broadway
New York, NY 10012

89 90 91 92 93 / 5 4 3 2 1

Haynes, Karen S.
    Women managers in human services / Karen S. Haynes.
        p.   cm. — (Springer series on social work ; vol. 15)
    Bibliography: p.
    Includes index.
    ISBN 0-8261-5860-9
    1. Women social workers—United States—Promotions. 2. Human services—United States—Administration. 3. Women executives—United States. 4. Career development—United States. I. Title.
    II. Series: Springer series on social work ; v. 15.
    HV40.46.H39   1989
    331.4'813613'0973—dc19   89-5981
                                                                    CIP

Printed in the United States of America

To Jim -

whose enthusiasm of women's abilities helped birth this idea
whose support of the project nurtured its development
whose creative talents matured its perspective
whose patience brought it to resolution
whose love sustained me.

Contents

Foreword

Why does a book addressed to women in management in social work need to be written at all? Are women not in the majority in this profession? Was the profession not, in fact, founded primarily by women? Women have always excelled in this field and they continue to excel. Social work is a profession that stands out because it has afforded women many opportunities in society when other professions did not provide any access at all. Why then this book for women?

This book had to be written and must be read by men and women in social work because women do face special and unique problems in this profession. Women in social work are making gains within the structures and organizations where social work is practiced today and many women are moving into positions of managerial responsibility and national leadership. This book addresses the key issues that they face and provides insights useful to them as they develop and grow in their careers.

After all, we must remember that one of the advantages of social work is that it is a profession that fosters and encourages self awareness and self critique. It is also future oriented and embraces change. The ideals of social work require us to strive toward justice and to nourish individuals in their chosen paths. These ideals impel us to begin at home. If we can set a high standard of professionalism, equality, and contribution, other men and women will want to learn our "secret" and will want to join us.

It is therefore important to pave the way for women in social work and to provide them with the knowledge and supports they will need to fulfill the challenges of the leadership roles that they will occupy in ever higher numbers. The knowledge of topics such as career planning, mentoring, and networking will help to pave the way. We may, in fact, be the first profession which achieves a high standard of gender and racial equality in our age—an accomplishment different from the seeming equality, for women at least, in the early days of the profession. At that time women were often dominant yet they led social movements and loosely integrated "out-groups" bringing pressure on the dominant (and male-oriented) institutions of those times.

The greater challenge today is to lead within institutionalized human services organizations and other structures without abandoning the ideals associated with the change-oriented critiques of the past. We are, as women, no longer "on the outside looking in"—today we face a different reality. We are now, or soon will be, equal partners in the process. The last barriers, those discussed in this book, to equality within this profession will soon be gone—from that point on we may be in the business of aiding women in other professions to achieve in their spheres what they will be able to observe in ours.

Actions indeed speak louder than words. The words in these pages can instruct future action. I am convinced that Karen Haynes has written a valuable book, a book that will serve to guide our course and increase our commitment to the responsible leadership that will be sorely needed in the years ahead.

MARTHA S. WILLIAMS
Dean
School of Social Work
University of Texas at Austin

Preface

The rationale for this book is to sensitize women to the potential barriers which exist within organizations, within themselves, and within colleagues as they enter or move upward in human service management. This book also aims to provide explanations and prescriptions for preventing these problems or overcoming these barriers.

Despite the fact that social work has traditionally been viewed as a female profession, women have decreased proportionately in administrative positions in social work agencies over the past several decades. Multiple explanations exist, including internal and external barriers, the lack of mentoring and networking, the omission of career planning, and the differences in management style between men and women. But much less attention has been directed toward the development and articulation of strategies to deal with these persistant and pervasive problems. If the profession is to see an increase of women in human service management, human service organizations and women themselves need to be informed, trained, and prepared for negotiating these hurdles.

The intent of this book is not to blame or lecture, but through scenarios, case illustrations, and a review of relevant literature, to frame the issues. Emphasis will be given to developing strategies for women in management to become more sophisticated in identifying potential barriers, to equip themselves with skills and techniques to enter management competitively, and to better negotiate the managerial hierarchy.

What is abundantly clear in the present social work management literature is the continued lack of attention to managerial issues and problems as they affect women differently. Texts continually omit content, case illustrations, or strategies relating to women's issues and perspectives in human service management. Articles directed at managerial strategies for women are scattered, not focused on a central theme and consequently, not easily accessible to female students or practitioners. Although schools seldom have entire courses devoted to women in management, this book could easily be utilized as a secondary text in an administrative behavior class, a supervision class, or even an organizational theory course. It seems obvious that there is a need for this type of book and the readership should include both social work students and social work practitioners.

Chapter 1 will provide a general overview of the essential topics and issues. Chapter 2 will describe in greater detail the external and internal barriers which women in human service management have experienced. Chapter 3 provides much needed career planning information and strategies. Chapter 4 focuses on Job Search issues and strategies.

The importance of mentoring and networking in career development are the central concepts in Chapters 5 and 6. Chapter 7 includes the elements of managerial style and Chapter 8 wrestles with false myths surrounding women, high technology, and high finance. Lastly, Chapter 9 addresses the complex issues of balancing career, friends, and family and provides some summary prescriptions.

Acknowledgments

This book is the product of many associations with very special people during my lifetime. First and foremost, my mother, the first woman manager I knew. She and her generation were the superwomen, trying to be everything to everyone.

Additionally, along the way, there have been some extremely important friends and mentors who have shared, modeled, discussed, and lamented many of these issues. Marta Westall, Karen Holmes, and Martha Williams with their talents, concern, and sense of humor remain constant reminders of the best of "women in management."

There have been a multitude of female graduate students whose interest in this topic and support to continue this project kept me going even as my managerial role expanded and almost overwhelmed me. Shelley Baute, for one, through her interest in communication styles directed me in new areas of investigation. Certainly, the first graduate seminar which I taught on women in management in human services at Indiana University provided insights and solutions beyond my own.

Specific talents and supports more recently have come from Kimberli Williams and Sheri Golly, secretary and graduate assistant, whose efforts went beyond the descriptions of their jobs. Certainly, the laboratory of a managerial position has given me illustrations and much cause for contemplation throughout the production of this manuscript.

Women Managers
in Human Services

1 Women in Social Work

Sheila, a middle-level administrator, sits at her desk gazing at a rather large pile of mail. As she begins the daily chore of mail review, a wave of discontent comes over her. She has held her current position for six years and although she likes it, the early challenges have dimmed and she often thinks of moving on. However, she is not confident that she has the skills and abilities to move into a higher-level management position.

As she plows through the mail, she reaches a letter from Marsha, a friend in another city. Attached to the letter is a job announcement, with a note: "Looks like a perfect job for you. Why don't you go for it?" Marsha, more of a mentor than a friend, is a real go-getter—who continuously encourages Sheila to seek a higher administrative position. As she reads the job announcement, a lack of self-confidence sweeps over her. The position is executive director of a large family service agency in a major metropolitan area. The agency has six satellite offices with a $1.5 million dollar budget and a staff of 47 employees. Although Sheila's current position includes supervision of 20 staff persons and responsibility for a half-million dollar budget, she still feels not ready to take this step. The $57,000 salary is attractive, but Sheila cannot help questioning whether she is "worth it."

Marsha often has told her that she should have a career plan formulated. For years, Sheila has moved from one agency to another and has changed positions within the current agency without a long-term career plan in mind. Quite clearly this position is something that she has dreamed about. She places the announcement on her desk and begins to reflect on the hassles and the tedium of her present job. She finds herself immediately discounting the possibility that she could get the offer. After all, she does not know the organization's staff and she is a woman—everybody knows these kinds of positions are given to men.

She sighs in resignation. It also would mean uprooting her family to move to another community.

She stands and walks to the window, remembering her last conversation with Marsha. "Never decide on whether you want a job until they offer it to you," Marsha said. "Always keep your options open." She knows Marsha is right and that at least she should apply for the job. She returns to her desk to reread the job announcement.

Sheila knows she would enjoy the larger community and already has extensive experience in family service agencies. The job announcement indicates that knowledge of budgets and creative fundraising are required, a description that perplexes Sheila. She recalls the time she applied for a position with a local agency. She knew she had been well-qualified and competent to fill the position. In fact, she was so confident that her past experience and skills were so strong—and others agreed—that she believed she needed only to apply to be offered the position. However, the position was not offered. She remembers, with anger, that she was not part of the "good old boy" system. In fact, during the job interview she was asked specifically how she would handle family responsibilities along with heavy professional ones. Her frustration and anger at being asked this question hampered her ability to proceed smoothly in the interview. The disappointment and anger upon finding that a man, less experienced and less competent, had been hired kept her from seeking higher positions.

Discouragement and disappointment hit Sheila again. She looked at the list of the Search and Screen Committee members and noted who was chair. All but two were men. She heard herself ask, "Why bother?" She crumpled the job announcement and threw it in the waste basket.

* * *

This scenario is by no means an atypical illustration of the barriers and problems, internal as well as external, that face women in management or women aspiring to managerial positions each day. Even more unfortunately, as the social work profession has increased in numbers and matured in skill and experience, the numbers of women in administrative positions has decreased. Not only do these barriers continue to exist, but both educational and service delivery organizations continue to ignore, or worse yet, deny, their existence and consequently provide no skills in anticipating and overcoming these barriers.

THE STATUS OF WOMEN IN SOCIAL WORK

Historically and traditionally, social work has been known primarily as a female profession. Over time, women have held all the jobs within the profession from top leadership positions in social work to direct service positions. Women pioneered the field of social work, breaking the trail for social work to have a role in many new areas of human services. The trend thus far has been for females to initiate new program areas only to be replaced later by males in the leadership position. As practice evolves, the leadership changes from female to male in disproportionate number (Kravitz, 1976; Sutton, 1982; York, Henley, & Gamble, 1987). Despite the fact that two-thirds of the social work profession is composed of females, male social workers dominate the administrative positions (Fanshel, pp. 448–454, 1976; Srinika & Chess, 1983). This two-thirds that Fanshel refers to is somewhat misleading as it underrepresents the actual number of women who perform social work jobs and functions, but who lack a formal social work education.

Other studies indicate that the female:male ratio in administration appears to be decreasing. In fact, one survey of over 800 agencies showed that the percentage of female executives had decreased from 60% in 1957 to 16% in 1976. A study of national social service organizations revealed that over the last several decades men have replaced women in administrative positions at a rate of 2% per year (Szakacs, 1977). This underrepresentation of women in social work leadership has occurred through a variety of discriminatory practices against women in relation to salaries, promotions, job opportunities, and task allocations—even when variables such as career tenure, education, family status, family commitment, and job mobility were controlled. Williams, Ho, and Fielder concluded their study with these comments, "in general the results seem to suggest that professional women do not receive lower salaries because of family obligations, inadequate education, less career experience, or part-time work. Rather the results indicate that women seem to fare badly in the promotion-division structure" (Williams, Ho, & Fielder, p. 466, 1974; Chernesky, 1980; York, Henley, & Gamble, 1985, 1987).

The resultant lack of women in top management further exacerbates the problem because there are few female role models and mentors. Whenever a woman does achieve a top administrative position, she often is the only female at that level and may be viewed as atypical and "token." Too often, a woman administrator may become less effective as a result of the stress of the "superwoman syndrome" and the lack of peer support. Not surprisingly, younger women who perceive these problems or barriers may not aspire to these positions.

The problem of few women in top positions, however, is not unique to social work. Statistics report that this is true in all other professions in the United States. What is relatively unique to social work is the fact that most professionals are female and the profession itself has been pioneered by women and their efforts (Shann, 1983; Collins, 1984; Talbot, & Bachrach, 1985). Famous for their contributions are women such as Mary Richmond,

Jane Addams, the Abbott sisters, and Florence Kelly. A great deal of speculation of why men prevail in the leadership roles was written in the 1970s. These works addressed possible variables and forms of discrimination that may have contributed to perpetuating the problem.

One important explanation, repeatedly suggested, may be arrived at by examining the 1940s and 1950s when social work was concerned with its "professional image." At that time an attempt was made to recruit men into the field. Chafetz described this process as "an effort to de-feminize social work; that is, make it more intellectual, rational, scientific and administrative—in short give it more male qualities" (Chafetz, p. 18, 1972; Collins, 1986). Men entered social work and, within this primarily female profession, continued to reflect the rest of the world by influencing arenas of social work practice whose activities were most consistent with the traditional male role such as community organization and administration. A division in the performance of social work functions, based on traditional sex roles, thus became firmly established (Kravitz, 1976). As Scotch noted, "high ranking occupations in all societies are typically male. For all occupations in all societies as one approaches the top, the proportion of men increases and the proportion of women decreases" (Scotch, p. 7, 1971; Collins, 1984; Tickamyer & Boke-Meier, pp. 336–337, 1984).

In social work from the 1950s until the present, males and females have performed different functions and, consequently, their status and salaries have divided on similar lines (Bakke & Edson, 1977; Curlee & Raymond, 1978). Men not only move into management positions more quickly than women, but they also move out of initial direct-service positions twice as often as women, indicating that men move into administrative-support and supervisory positions early in their careers and at a much faster rate than women (Valentich & Gripton, 1978; Jennings & Daley, 1979). The fact that men choose the administrative track in disproportionate numbers is not due to gender differences in professional aspirations, but to differential recruitment (Diangson, Kravetz, & Lipton, 1975; Berkun, 1984; York, Henley, & Gamble, 1985). Male students reportedly have more contact with their professors and advisors; have more relaxed and informal relations with faculty; have more invitations to co-author papers; and attend professional conferences and meet members of the field. This seems to suggest that sex-role stereotyping and differential opportunities affect vital aspects of social work students' educational experience (Stafford, 1987).

Adding to this are data indicating that the percentage of male members of NASW, which had risen to 43% by the 1960s, has dropped to 28% by the mid-1980s. During that same period, the proportion of social workers in administrative roles dropped from 50 to 30% (Sarri, 1987).

THE ISSUES FOR WOMEN

The issues for women in, or entering, administration in social work clearly are as complex as the historical progression and the current status would suggest. These issues range from organizational barriers, both formal and informal; to educational gaps in the socialization and skill preparation for female students; to behavioral characteristics; to career strategies.

Organizational barriers may lie in the formal organizational structure or in the attitudes and behaviors of others. These represent not only barriers to entrance into managerial positions, but act as impediments to upward mobility once an entry-level managerial position is gained. Formal barriers can be descriptions of job qualifications that require previous administrative experience or specialized skills, which only an "insider" can have, or they can be the allocation of tasks to women that do not require teamwork, provide visibility, or introduce new skills. Informal barriers include the absence of a cohesive peer group, supervision that is too direct and controlling, or collegial attitudes that do not take women managers seriously.

While these organizational barriers have been reflected in the literature, strategies for successfully overcoming them have not been described. Women's socialization, education, and management training may, indeed, focus on perceiving some barriers to be desirable. For example, women frequently are not given credit for work accomplished in groups, so individualized task assignment may seem desirable and be prescribed. The difficulty is that women may not perceive that individualized tasks may not provide them the team work, visibility, and networking that also are essential elements to upward mobility and organizational success.

Educational issues also exist, which act as impediments to women aspiring to, or achieving, managerial positions. Despite the inclusion since 1977 in the Council on Social Work Education's Standards to require curricular attention to women's content, management curriculum in both class and field falls short in providing strategies and models for women students to move into and within management positions. Special courses, or even identifiable course topics, on women in management areas are sparse; female administrators for field instruction and role models are few as are female classroom instructors.

While it is often suggested that women's socialization more than likely emphasizes feminine traits such as nurturance, passivity, dependence, and other-directedness, women also are likely to be protected from exposure, discouraged from risk-taking, and unaccustomed to being held responsible for the results of their actions. They often have less opportunity for team play and to learn leadership roles. This leads, more importantly, to giving them little self-confidence and a low self-concept in meeting management role expectations. The lack of team playing often has resulted in women not knowing how to work collegially, being more comfortable with individualized task assignments, and not knowing the game rules.

Career planning, an essential and multifaceted project, takes on exaggerated importance for women aspiring to administrative and management positions. Given women's reported predilection for attributing success to luck, this is a misconception that must be eradicated.

Women aspiring to administration must acknowledge that it is acceptable to pursue a career. The literature suggests that the more techniques one applies to job hunting, the less luck is a factor in job success. Explanations for the lack of career planning by women relate to a combination of factors more unique to women's lives and socialization. For example, women make late career decisions and often treat employment as a series of jobs, rather than as a career. Women may place more emphasis on personal self-improvement rather than on career and skill improvement. Furthermore, women have a sense of passivity in career decisions and tend to attribute success to luck.

The job search itself is a critical step in the successful attainment of upward mobility. Once again, preparedness and assertiveness are essential ingredients.

The lack of mentors and role models in administration for women represents an important and pervasive difficulty that women historically have faced and continue to face. Given the aforementioned statistics on the proportion of women in administration in social work agencies and in social work education, clearly few women will have direct contact with managerial women as mentors and role models. Much of the literature on mentoring suggests that successful men, fast-track men, and "smart" men have mentors. It is within these relationships that junior-level men learn the informal organizational rules, the appropriate game strategy, and the path to the fast track and gain the necessary experiences and relationships to move upward. Also, what is simpler for the junior-level male with a senior-level male mentor is the nonexistence of sexual innuendos within the relationship.

Networking, a widespread and much-discussed strategy, also is less commonly utilized by women. Women often confuse support groups and informal work relationships with the more formalized and purposive aspects of networking. While many women have support groups to fulfill emotional needs or have close working relationships with colleagues, they often fail in networking, which involves individuals at one's level or beyond whose knowledge, skills, and experience are useful for career mobility. Networking usually is described as occurring outside of one's organization and, therefore, can be useful in gaining knowledge about other jobs and information about how other organizations structure task assignments in the organizational hierarchy.

Managerial style can positively or negatively affect one's leadership effectiveness and should be purposively studied and evaluated. Since gender differences exist in communication patterns and managerial styles, an understanding of these styles and their impact on superiors, colleagues, and subordinates is important.

Too often, women are criticized for an inability or aversion to high technology and high finance in the workplace. Such myths must be exploded and appropriate strategies employed.

Finally, balancing career demands with personal interests and demands is the struggle of all administrators, but are more salient concerns for female administrators. The managerial woman must accept the impossibility of the "superwoman syndrome" and must set realistic limitations.

CREATING THE FUTURE

In conclusion it should be evident that there are an array of barriers—perceived or real—that can prohibit the entrance of women into managerial-educational tracks, entry-level managerial jobs, or higher-level managerial jobs. The first steps in overcoming these barriers must be knowledge of their existence, the ability to identify them accurately, and then implementing an assortment of strategies to overcome them.

Since the proportion of women entering social work education and administrative tracks within social work education continues to be high, it is evident that in the future there will be increasing pools of talented women.

2 Overcoming Barriers to Advancement

Sheila has just left her boss's office. Confused, she begins to sift through the discussion for clarity. He had said that she was doing an excellent job and that he was delighted with her report on the need for additional staff in her unit, to be presented to the United Way allocation panel.

Yet, he also told her that she had been passed by for a promotion. He said that she "was not ready yet"; that she had not been with the agency long; and that she already had moved up quite quickly. He also noted, "I thought that you were happy at your present level—you certainly are doing an excellent job there."

A mixture of feelings floods over Sheila. Was seeking a promotion not to be expected? Had she not received a high merit increment for last year's excellent performance? Had she not taken on several additional tasks at the last minute, thinking that this was an expected part of playing the game?

Anger comes next. Why did Pete get the promotion? Perhaps she was disadvantaged because she often made tasks seem easy, rather than admit that she did not have enough information, access, skill, or time to complete them adequately. Perhaps the after-hours drinks were more than social get-togethers. Why had no one prepared her to realize that some of her colleagues, superiors, and subordinates might resent a woman's fast track?

Frustration follows. How would the next time be different? If doing all the jobs assigned, doing them well, and playing by the rules did not work, what did? Whom could she ask?

* * *

INTRODUCTION

Sheila's problems are neither idiosyncratic nor a phenomenon of the past. They face women in social work today at many critical junctures in their educational preparation and throughout their careers.

As noted in the introductory chapter, women have decreased proportionately in administrative positions in social work agencies, even though social work traditionally has been viewed as a female profession. Discrimination with respect to salaries, promotions, and job opportunities continues to prevail in the social work profession (Scotch, 1971; Knapman, 1977; Jennings & Daley, 1979). While these are critical issues, what happens to women who have attained managerial status has not been explored (Hanlan, 1977; Chernesky, 1983; Austin, Karvetz, & Pollock, 1985).

In organizations in which men continue to have vested interest and control, the decision to accept women as executives is frequently not a voluntary choice. Men sometimes still have difficulty in accommodating the legal requirement to provide equal opportunity and there is a good deal of behind-the-scene manipulations to avoid fulfilling this requirement. For example, employers, male as well as female, ask questions of women that they simply would not put to men: "What does your spouse do? Do you have a family? Do you have help at home? How do you feel about traveling alone?" These questions are not only illegal, they are an affront to any sincere and capable woman executive.

There are male executives who are more forthright in their acceptance of women as colleagues, or at least think that they are. However, such men cannot quite figure out how to utilize women in the organization. So, they ask questions such as, "Will men take orders from a woman? Can women be as aggressive and objective as men? Will women need to have special job assignments? Should women be slotted into soft managerial functions like personnel, public relations, long-term strategic planning, instead of finance, marketing, and fundraising?"

These concerns about appropriate managerial roles for women are further compounded by male belief in myths about women such as biological handicaps, decision making based on feelings, rather than facts; an inability to commit themselves to work because of spouse or children, and so on. Contrary to these myths, declining numbers of women leave the labor force for marriage and children and, of those who do, the majority return to full-time, long-term employment as soon as their children enter school. Furthermore, studies indicate that differences in turnover between men and women are small (Bureau of Labor Statistics, 1983). That is to say as workforce participants women are as permanent and stable as men.

BARRIERS

When women's progress is impeded within the promotional hierarchy, in large part, it is due to either personal or organizational barriers or a combination of them. It is essential that these barriers be perceived, understood, and anticipated if possible and that strategies, organizational and personal, for overcoming them be developed and instituted. Barriers, real or perceived, overt or covert, hinder progress toward the achievement of managerial and leadership opportunities for women. In the following discussion, these barriers are categorized as those that are external and those internal to women.

External Barriers

External barriers to upward mobility are those outside the woman herself; they are within the environment, in the organizational structure, or in the attitudes and behaviors of others. Opportunities within an organization or professional association can be differentially constrained by task assignments, positional descriptions, personnel practices, relationships among peers and subordinates, and communication networks (Calkin, 1983; Kravitz & Austin, 1984). Previous research has indicated that women often are channeled into jobs and positions that offer little visibility, mobility, or influence. This channeling can occur through a set of structural barriers— organizational barriers—consisting of institutional policies, procedures, and patterns that often place women managers at a disadvantage. These structural barriers may well represent the most obvious and most significant set of barriers, and they are readily observed and studied. However they are, by no means, already redressed by organizations. These barriers are: (1) job qualifications and job descriptions; (2) task description and assignment; (3) evaluative mechanisms for performance; (4) the distribution of benefits. Each of these is discussed below. A fifth, less obvious external barrier, organizational relationships, will also be covered.

Job Qualifications

While organizations are increasingly sensitive to affirmative action related to hiring, there is great latitude within the same job title and job qualifications. It is erroneous to believe that simply because jobs are labeled similarly on an organizational chart that tasks, responsibilities, and authority are identical. Consequently, where these differences exist, differential opportunities and access to information and power are likely to follow.

Job qualifications are quite obviously the first place in which subtle, but powerful, discrimination can occur. Administrative positions that require

such applicant credentials as "prior administrative experience" can effectively keep competent and aspiring women out of management through a
"catch-22" philosophy. That is, women cannot be qualified to compete for a
management job without management experience and they do not get the
opportunity to have management experience. Clearly urging organizations
to rewrite job qualifications to include administrative experience or its
equivalent, or better yet, administrative potential is desirable (Shein, 1973;
Stewart & Gudykunst, 1982).

However, even when these overt qualifications are reconciled, research
demonstrates that when males and females are considered for the same
administrative positions, subtle differences in necessary attributes may be
imposed (Cecil, Paul, & Olins, 1973; Rosen & Jerdee, 1974, 1978). For
example, women are seen to need qualifications for administrative positions
that fall into categories of personality/appearance and skills/education,
whereas men are seen to need motivational abilities and interpersonal/
relations skills. The implication here is that the same administrative job
might be subtly defined as different for men than for women, which consequently suggests that different skills are prioritized. Consider the following vignette.

Recently the male chair of a search and screen committee telephoned a
female executive as a reference for a former female administrative employee,
currently an applicant for an executive director's position. He explained that
the primary tasks involved public relations, fundraising, and providing community leadership in the prevention of child abuse. The executive spoke
highly of the employee's past experience, her previous fundraising skills, her
articulate presentation style, and her skills in leadership. The chairperson
paused and then said that several members of the search and screen committee—not himself—were concerned because the applicant was quite overweight. When the female executive asked why weight was relevant to the
job qualifications, the chairperson reiterated that it was not his issue and that
he was unconcerned.

Style and appearance may wield their influence in executive decisions
more often for women than for men. Being overweight (or petite) may be
used against a woman, but being large may be viewed as "having a presence"
for a man.

Task Assignment

Task assignment and allocation are other important organizational activities
that can either constrain or promote women's managerial progress. The
literature suggests that women may be assigned to tasks that prevent, rather
than enhance, the development of expertise; that place them in individualized and invisible positions within an organization; and that contribute

more to organizational maintenance than to organizational growth (Mai-Dalton & Sullivan, 1981).

Unfortunately, the concern that women's work on team or group projects often goes unnoticed or unrewarded has spurred many women to doggedly pursue independent tasks. While the rewards and benefits of individualized tasks are clear, the inability to work in a team or on a group project can be detrimental. Organizational politics is teamwork and leaders must have supportive followers. Consequently, organizations must purposively assign tasks to women which include interdependent as well as independent tasks.

The assignment of women solely or predominantly to organizational maintenance tasks such as personnel management or staff supervision, rather than to organizational growth tasks such as project development or fundraising, further restrains their upward mobility. Although organizational maintenance tasks are essential to every organization, they tend to be routine, not demand skill enhancement, and provide limited visibility for the employee within and outside the organization. Maintenance tasks are "nontransitional" tasks; that is, they do not force the employee to learn new skills that are necessary for a higher-level managerial position.

It is desirable for all organizational members to have well-defined tasks, but task ambiguity may be especially problematic for women. If the task is not well-defined, norms governing task completion, division of labor, and authority and accountability may not be either. Women managers are purportedly more dissatisfied with the lack of clarity of goals and tasks than are men. This is likely explained because many female managers are outside the informal communication network and consequently lack informal clarity as well (Kerson & Alexander, 1979; Haynes, 1983).

Evaluation

Related to, but not entirely dependent upon, task clarity are objective evaluative mechanisms within the organization. When tasks are ambiguously defined, haphazardly assigned, and not viewed as "growth" related, mechanisms and opportunities for evaluation may be less than routinized, formalized, and objective. Since positive evaluation of performance is essential for upward mobility and for increasing self-confidence, it can be another important barrier for women. For example, chairing "standing committees" in agencies, such as grievance committees, or editing the agency's newsletter are tasks never completed, not highly valued, and often without objective outcome measures. How does one evaluate the success of a grievance committee? By the number of grievances filed? Or, by a specific outcome, such as a grievance denied?

Beyond the difficulty in specificity of task, is the delineation of time intervals for evaluation. The informal "Trust me. I'll tell you if you are not progressing well," can be extremely detrimental to women. Routine, formal evaluations, if they do not occur, do not become part of the individual's personnel record, cannot be forwarded to a new job, and in formal evaluations, cease to exist once the immediate supervisor moves on.

If, in addition, male managerial style is used as an evaluative mechanism, women undoubtedly suffer discrimination in performance evaluation. How often she talks in a staff meeting, rather than what she says, may be used as an evaluative criteria. Conformity to norms such as business lunches and Friday social hours can enter the informal and unwritten evaluation.

Benefits

Salary usually is noted to be differentially and inequitably distributed between male and female employees even when such factors as job tenure, education, part-time employment, marital status, and family obligations are controlled (Williams, Ho, & Fiedler, 1974; Fanshel, 1976; Rubin, 1982; Yamatani, 1982). Salary differentials also exist when job titles are identical. However, salary is not usually a barrier to upward mobility.

Explanations for why women are not promoted as frequently as men may be partially explained by examining how other benefits are distributed. These benefits include short leaves to attend conferences and workshops; reimbursements for tuition and travel per diem for conferences and workshops; and extended educational leave to complete a degree or a certificate. While viewed as organizational symbols of reward, such benefits also are extremely necessary for the attainment of new skills, for networking, and for visibility, all of which enhance the possibility for upward mobility within or across organizations (Jennings & Daley, 1979).

Also included among these benefits are organizational practices related to flex-time and part-time opportunities, maternity leave, and child care. Unfortunately, social service agencies, like the corporate sector, have failed to establish fair and nondiscriminatory practices in these areas. Social service agencies are beset by employee turnover, which creates costly needs for constant in-service training of new employees. Therefore, while not the only explanation, the absence of these organizational benefits certainly contributes to turnover, at the same time prohibiting continuous employment and skill building for women. In many social service agencies today, sick leave cannot be utilized for dependent care and flex-time does not exist.

Organizational Attitudes Toward Women

In management, myths such as women are useless with numbers, unable to balance budgets, too emotional to make objective decisions, or not serious about their careers can be serious impediments to achieving a management position or a promotion (Schein, 1973; Noe, 1988). These subtle forms of sexism are certainly as damaging as the more overt structural barriers. Women, new to management roles and the board room, constantly are faced with behaviors that can be labeled chivalrous or paternalistic, but that also are almost always debilitating.

Some of these behaviors may be utilized unconsciously or because they are the only behaviors men know with respect to women. Many men have experienced women predominantly in one of three basic sets of roles: those concerning family, sexuality, or rivalry (Chafetz, 1978). In family roles, men believe that women are nurturers and have a willingness to be dominated. The female administrator who is younger than her male counterparts or superiors often is placed in the role of daughter. Men treat her with a protective attitude. She is prevented from entering a situation or taking on a responsibility that is "too difficult." Often because they believe that it is "in your best interest" to be protected, these men refuse to see the sexism and discrimination that occurs from paternalism.

A female administrator who shows gentleness and understanding and is as old as or older than her male colleagues or superior is categorized as the "motherly" type. Usually, mother is not seen as a competent, directive, assertive administrator, but is the organizational healer of "family feuds," a role extremely draining, but not organizationally rewarded by promotions. The last of the family roles is that of homemaker/hostess—the coffee maker or note taker. This role effectively reduces women's abilities to serve in other more important roles, while simultaneously reducing their status in the eyes of others.

The second set of roles into which women in the workplace can be placed is sex roles. Viewing a woman as "a tease" or "a piece" clearly suggests the narrow and degraded image of women that some men have and which, translated into the workplace, militates against an attitude of seriousness and respect. The continued existence of sexual harrassment on the job and the persistence of the "blaming the victim" mentality are demonstrations of this role set. Another sex role in which some men place women in the workplace is that of "babymaker." The concerns voiced during an application process or in a promotional interview involving potential pregnancy, maternity leaves, or worse yet, discontinuation of her career emanate from this role set. Women with children constantly are queried during job interviews or in preparation for business travel about how they will handle child care.

The third role set involves rival roles. In these roles, the woman is viewed as an intruder and an interloper. She is, worse yet, seen as abandoning her ascribed role as wife and mother. One rival role is that of "rookie," in which the woman must be tested and retested to prove herself worthy of the position. She is often subjected to crude jokes and sports analogies by "the boys," who test how she reacts to the "man's world." She also may be given unrealistic tasks that she is unable to perform. After a rookie completes her basic training, she then may be typecast as a "dumb broad"—less intelligent and less organized than her male peers if she chooses not to be overtly assertive and competitive. If she behaves assertively and knowledgeably, she may then be labeled a "bitch." An upwardly mobile young man is respectfully called a "fast tracker," the young woman with the same ambition is labeled a "castrator."

Unfortunately, the management world is full of differential descriptions such as "he's careful about details; she's picky." And, "he exercises authority; she's tyrannical." A woman executive can be labeled as "autocratic" because she made an administrative decision. Conversely, she "abdicates responsibility and authority" when she asks for employee input.

It is far more difficult to identify strategies clearly to overcome these attitudinal barriers, which create discriminatory and sexist behaviors and practices. The first step is to identify these attitudes, not respond to them, thereby conforming to the role of the petulant daughter or the nurturing wife. Organizations must continue to create other models of organizational and work roles, with which men can relate to women. Organizations need to identify and label behaviors and attitudes that are sexist and that create the "chilly" and harrassing organizational climates in which women find themselves.

Enacting or monitoring policies such as flex-time, parental leave, and sick leave for dependent care offer all organizational employees the opportunity to discover that personal obligations are not mutually exclusive of professional career choices. Orientation for new or newly promoted employees should include as much specificity as possible regarding dress codes, informal socialization norms, and average promotional tracks.

Organizational policies may not need to be changed, but practices may need to be initiated to increase gender-free roles. For example, minute taking or coffee making for meetings can become rotated responsibilities. And, volunteering for a difficult or risky task can be shared equally by staff.

Internal Barriers

Frequently, psychological barriers, or internal factors, are used to explain why women fail to become administrators. Attitudes, aspirations, or behaviors of women themselves can inhibit them from moving into management and affect their performance (Kravitz & Jones, 1982).

Socialization

While women's socialization emphasizes traits such as nurturance, passivity, dependence, and other-directedness, women are also likely to be protected from exposure and discouraged from risk-taking. They may also be un-accustomed to being held responsible for their actions. And, they may have less opportunity for team play and to learn leadership roles (Wong, Ket-tlewell, & Sproule, 1985). Given that much of management requires asser-tiveness, self-direction, risk-taking, and team play, women quite logically have less self-confidence and lower self-concepts to meet management role expectations.

Women's socialization usually includes heavy doses of "niceness orientation." Nice girls are quiet, helpful, and agreeable. The difficulty in saying no to unreasonable demands or expectations or to task or job assign-ments that do not extend one's potential seems to permeate female adminis-trators' concerns and wreak havoc with professional calendars and multiple obligations. Saying no feels selfish and induces guilt in women; yet saying no to the right requests frees the administrator to allocate time to those tasks most important not only to the organization but to her own professional growth.

Fear of Success

The "fear of success" syndrome has generated a great deal of controversy. This theory suggests that women actually avoid success because they are afraid it will make them less feminine, or make others perceive them as less feminine (Horner, 1969; Treasmar, 1974; Hyland, Curtis, & Mason, 1985).

Although the theory and its attendant behaviors have been contested, two related tendencies do seem to exist: (1) women are less likely to expect to succeed than are men and (2) when women do succeed, they are more likely to attribute their success to external factors (i.e. luck) than to their own competency. Women continually explain job successes by saying, "I was in the right place at the right time. I was lucky."

Interestingly, in the human services, professional theories and clinical techniques seem focused upon and invested in helping clients to become "self-determining." This assumes that the attitudes, behaviors, and self-concepts taught to our clients will be self-fulfilling and more importantly, that one should be able to influence and control one's own life.

Women need to incorporate this concept. If women believe, act, and feel that they will be successful, they have a far better chance of becoming so. Too many women hesitate to "brag" on a resume, in a letter of applica-tion, or in a job interview. How can women convince others of their abilities and potentials if they do not believe in themselves? How can women expect others to put confidence in their abilities by promoting them, hiring them, and giving them increasing responsibilities if they appear unable to fulfill these responsibilities?

Additionally, not only are women fearful of success, they often experience guilt and ambivalence upon achieving it. Guilt is associated with their inability to attribute success to talent and, consequently, some women feel guilty that they have succeeded too easily or too quickly. Furthermore, if they have outdone Dad, their boss, or their spouse, the guilt may be exacerbated.

Although it is a cliche, the saying that "nothing succeeds like success" deserves attention. Women should remove the term *luck* from their vocabulary and be able to accept and explain successes by talent, hard work, planning, and networking, rather than attributing success to luck, fate, or accident. While luck may occur in some situations, the ability to see the opportunity and link that opportunity to talent is by no means a "lucky" ability. If one believes that success is attributable to luck, one can neither take pride in what one has accomplished nor believe that success will continue.

Role Modeling

Women also must let go of the association between male characteristics and management style. An unfortunate illustration involves criticism recently made by two male administrators that a female administrator's style was "too trusting and open." If women accept the definition of management as not to control or direct, but to facilitate, they may begin to realize that they are ideally suited to management. The very characteristics of nurturance and other-directedness, sometimes referred to pejoratively, are invaluable to successful management. Indeed, if women are to look at the onslaught in the 1970s of management training focusing on sensitivity training, interpersonal skills, and participatory management, they would see that organizations began to recognize deficits in their managers' abilities, particularly in the area of human relations.

The best managers, it might be argued, display a combination of traditional "female" and "male" characteristics that encompass technical abilities as well as "people orientation." To be warm and caring, to admit mistakes, and to praise subordinates are not signs of weak or poor management, but signs of outstanding leadership.

If communication styles differ by gender, women managers may find themselves in situations in which their style is "neither accepted nor respected" (Chernesky, 1983). Consequently, women aspiring to management positions need to be given examples of a variety of styles of interaction and communication that support the "feminine" style as legitimate and effective. Criteria for judging managerial competence and effectiveness should be applied equally to female and male managers and should emanate from a nonsexist perception of effective style. It can be easy to label female employees as less assertive, decisive, or spontaneous than their male peers until one remembers that exhibiting those very behaviors might be mislabeled as aggressive, stubborn, or flighty.

Another set of barriers relates to the need for, but absence of, significant women for role models and for informal communication and information. Not only are these role models in limited supply in the workplace (thus acting as an external barrier), but women managers are less likely to reach out and find, identify, request, or initiate these relationships (which acts as an internal barrier).

It is extremely useful for women trying to decide their interest in management, or actively aspiring to it, to have an informal network of women administrators who may help guide them through job choices, resume preparation, job interview skills, and on-the-job difficulties. This supportive network provides the assurance that conflicts, problems, and lack of preparedness are not solitary or idiosyncratic difficulties. It also may broaden the pool of potential mentors for women (Faver, Fox, & Shannon, 1983). A female mentor not only serves as a role model, but she can bring to the relationship a better understanding of the particular problems that a woman faces in management.

It has been found repeatedly that formal training and the right job still are not enough for upward mobility and "fast tracking." Special knowledge and "secret know-how" are largely learned from an experienced "pro," who must be either observed as she practices or readily available to advise directly. In all professions, competence is created by exposing the new professional to the tasks necessary for upward mobility and by coaching and feedback (Greiff & Munter, 1980).

Thus, the professional woman aspiring to a leadership position must go beyond her formal education and involve herself in the particular socialization structure necessary to career advancement. These include support and personal relationships, task assignments, information provision, opportunities for participation in decision making, and increased visibility.

Organizations can reward women's styles and socialization by overtly acknowledging the diversity of styles essential to effective leadership. Additionally, organizations can provide opportunities for mentoring or networking by allocating benefits that promote or support those functions.

CONCLUSIONS

In summary, since research and experience show the continued existence of internal as well as external barriers to women in human service management, it is essential that women not only acknowledge these barriers, but prepare themselves to overcome or diminish them.

It seems evident that women encounter problems associated with organizational life in different and often counterproductive ways than do their male colleagues. While a lack of experience, different socialization, and, perhaps, a lack of assertiveness may constrain a woman manager's mobility, organizational policies and practices, as well as the attitudes and behaviors of other organizational members continue to be external and usually subtle barriers. Organizations must be forced to become more gender-free and less reliant on traditional (i.e. masculine) policies and managerial stereotypes. The following chapters will focus in much greater detail on these barriers and on strategies for overcoming them.

3 Career Planning

Sheila picks up the telephone and discovers that it is Joe, her counterpart in another division of the agency. Joe excitedly says, "I have some news. Our executive director has just submitted his resignation." Sheila is surprised and annoyed that Joe always seems to know such news before she does. She attended the most recent program director's meeting last week; why was nothing mentioned?

She immediately thinks of her neglect to create a career plan. Her usual style is to wait for an opportunity to occur rather than plan for the next desired position. Should she have a long-range strategy?

The news from Joe raises many questions again. Sheila asks herself whether this is an appropriate time to seek the position of director of the agency. Would this provide her with the experience and skills needed to get where she ultimately wants to go? She shakes her head in confusion and, in frustration, asks, "I don't even know where I want to go. How do I know whether this is the right step?"

* * *

INTRODUCTION

As this scenario illustrates, career opportunities often catch women either unprepared to make a move or indecisive about making such a move. Probably the most crucial discovery in the area of career planning for women is that it is acceptable to pursue a career actively rather than merely hold a job (Henning & Jardin, 1977). While women have pursued careers for many years, only recently have their careers become accepted without controversy.

Career planning also may help with some of the barriers discussed in the previous chapter. Research comparing career characteristics of men and women has revealed interesting findings. For example, it was found that professional women do not earn lower salaries because of family obligations, less career experience, or the need for only part-time work. Rather, much of the monetary differences between women and men exist even when these conditions are identical, which suggests that women suffer in the promotional structure (Williams, Ho, & Fielder, 1974; Rubin, 1982; Yamatani, 1982). Combinations of internal and external barriers contribute to slowing women down in career moves.

Additionally, research reveals that many of the common excuses for women's slow movement up the organizational ladder are myths, not founded in the reality of the workplace. For example, the reality is that women change jobs less often than men and are less mobile and more stable than men in the workplace. Men are more apt to look for a better position outside the organization. Consequently, arguments that it is not cost-effective to train women for managerial positions because they will leave the organization are not based in reality. In fact, it may be women's loyalty to the organization combined with a greater fear of risk-taking that reduces the likelihood of their changing organizations to attain upward mobility. Thus, if more employers were willing to promote from within, women's strategies and skill would be more successful (Williams, Ho, & Fielder, 1974).

Career planning is especially important for women aspiring to administrative and management positions. Since they will increasingly compete with men for these positions, women must learn the appropriate and successful tactics for achieving their management goals. Of essential importance, as noted earlier, is that women must see their professional future not just as a series of jobs, but rather as a career path (Valentich & Gripton, 1978).

Obscuring and impeding this process for women in social work is the fact that career planning is not addressed in the social work literature. From an early age men are socialized in ways that prepare them to perform the steps of career advancement later with little or no need to consciously study, learn, and practice the steps leading to the top. For better or worse, most men perceive that they do not have a choice about whether to work. For professional men, not surprisingly, the obligation to have a job "for life" becomes enacted early on by their taking steps for career success—both financial and social. In contrast, for women today, there is a multiplicity of possible career and life choices, which offers them the luxury of choice. This luxury creates confusion, indecision, and delays in the career paths of women. The luxury of options becomes interpreted by men in the workplace as a lack of serious intent about career, a reduced importance in the necessity for a career, and, not surprisingly, a reduced planning for a career.

As earlier noted in Chapter 2, differential socialization, life experiences, and early education and job choices make the career patterns of women not only different from those of men, but less effective in the marketplace. The career patterns of many women include the following elements:

- Late career decisions
- Sense of passivity
- Inadequate internalization of successes
- Emphasis on personal self-improvement
- Reliance on formal organizational structures, with a deemphasis on informal relationships
- Different definitions of job and career
- Theme of vicarious independence
- Inadequate perception of career as an integral part of life
- Undeveloped concept of personal strategy in terms of team-playing, planning, and making required shifts in skills
- Unproductive way of perceiving risk
- Undeveloped ability to perceive and deal with cues regarding advantageous use of style and role choices

These elements are likely to retard women's movement into and upward once they are within management.

Many women make important life choices, such as whether to go to college and marry and bear children. Ironically, many of the women who carefully plan marriage, college, and family, allow themselves to fall into a job without a vision of the long-term goal.

CAREER PLANNING DEFINED

Career planning involves taking a long-term view of one's work life as opposed to short-term, "Band-Aid™" thinking and includes determining alternative means of action about one's plans. To professional men, career planning is routine; women are only now finding that such planning is essential. Career planning is useless unless one knows what one wants to do, at least for the immediate future (Bolles, 1985).

Career planning is a multifaceted project, involving not only an analysis of one's career goals, but of one's talents and interests. In career planning, one must acknowledge personal life choices such as marriage and children. One of the most difficult areas for women is deciding how to balance career with family. These areas need not be mutually exclusive, but they do represent choices and any choice has a set of consequences.

Career and life planning is ideally an ongoing, continuous process, not a single event done once and for all. It is a process of evolutionary planning that requires the direction of self-knowledge, including elements of one's past, present, and future (Bolles, 1985). There is a prevalent misconception that luck determines one's career opportunities. Although luck is an inherent part of pursuing a career, the role of luck decreases as planning increases.

Stages in Career Development

To do career planning, one needs to realize that there are stages in career development. Authors such as Dalton (1977) have differentiated the following four stages of career development:

1. Preparatory stage—education, in-service training, initial experience (first five years or ages 18–25).
2. Formation stage—fastest growth and promotions (10–15 years or ages 25–35/40).
3. Watershed stage—reassessment of goals and priorities (next 10 years or ages 35–45/50).
4. Negotiating the heights—increased financial and professional rewards (after age 45/50).

When examining these stages, it is obvious that to move successfully through them one must reassess goals, develop new skills, or perfect current skills. Once one accepts that career planning involves stages, one can understand that most careers start with staff positions or lower-level management jobs and require education and in-service training at several junctures. One also can recognize that upward mobility in management must follow an initiation or internship phase of "learning the rules" and "playing the game."

Since career planning also is done to move upward in management, not only is the initial definition of goals challenging, but there are transitional phases that offer unique challenges and opportunities as well. Sometimes, the focus is on "getting one's foot in the door," with the often mistaken assumption that movement will be easier or, at least, more defined once inside (Lee, 1980).

Too often, middle-management positions are inaccurately described in terms of tangible characteristics such as salary, fringe benefits, office size, or title. Such positions are seldom defined in terms of the actual on-the-job changes that accompany what is essentially a shift from supervisory management to a level of management that entails broader, across-department responsibilities. Yet an understanding of this shift is critical for the upwardly mobile professional: It helps the individual recognize what career path to take and what skills to develop to attain middle-management positions.

The typical management career path moves an individual from an initial role as a professional and specialized staffer to a more general role as a middle manager. To be more specific, the clinical expertise that may have been critical to obtaining the first-line supervisory position, now is relegated to a less critical role in securing the program director's position. From that point on, career paths involve a new type of specialization that requires increased conceptual approaches in organizational design, as well as skill in decision making and problem solving.

The function of the specialist staffer or supervisor is to apply specialized and technical knowledge and experience in solving primarily routine problems, so as to assure the completion of assigned tasks. Supervisory responsibilities at this level are closely related to task completion and the proper use of techniques and skills (Hennig & Jardin, 1977). So, for example, a supervisor of clinical staff in a residential-treatment facility will use an array of interpersonal skills to interact with the staff and rely on the therapeutic body of knowledge to assess each clinician's competence and assessment skills. However, the program director of the same residential facility will be concerned with staffing schedules and patterns, the cooperation of multidisciplinary staff, and the cost-effectiveness of service-delivery strategies. The director will leave the concern about specific treatment modalities to the clinicians and their supervisors.

Thus, the middle manager's job involves the coordination of functions with counterparts in other areas within the organization. This ensures that the work of her own department is effective relative to the immediate objectives and operations of the entire organization. Generally the catch for human service personnel is how to obtain the experience and expertise that facilitates the transition from a position requiring narrow and highly specialized clinical and management skills to a position that requires broader knowledge of management theory and techniques.

At top managerial levels, senior managers are much less involved than junior managers in seeing that work is completed, in meeting day-to-day requirements, or in coordinating operational interdependence between and among functional areas. Executives are much more closely involved in setting long-term directions and developing policies for entire functional areas in order to give coherence to the operations of the enterprise as a whole.

The point for women is this: If they enter organizations with aspirations that differ significantly from men's—that is, they are not certain about a lifelong career—then they cannot expect to move much beyond the formation stage of career development. For example, if women concentrate on the acquisition of competence in the skill areas of their current job, rather than on skill acquisition for future jobs, the transition to middle and upper management will be extremely difficult. To move beyond this stage, the barriers discussed earlier must be identified and overcome. Women must be given (or take on) tasks and assignments that provide broader base experience, skill enhancement, and organizational visibility.

CAREER PLANNING STEPS

In beginning to define or redefine a career plan, the first phase repeatedly identified is goal setting (Bolles, 1985; Buskirk, 1980; Figler, 1979). One common factor noted in the career planning of successful people is that in most cases they knew what they wanted—they had goals (Buskirk, 1980). A sequence for goal-directed behavior begins with a goal statement, then includes an assessment phase, which is followed by a strategy for action. The ingredients of career planning include the specific behavioral indices, the resources necessary for attainment, a timetable, and a method of measuring results.

Inherent to goal-directed behavior is the close inspection of one's desires, values, and skills. Goal setting is beneficial because it provides direction by which to make decisions surrounding multiple opportunities; it provides emotional peace of mind; and it provides a unit of measure by which to determine successes. Once an original goal is established, further areas must be addressed.

This need not be a lifetime, thirty-year goal, but it must be one that can effectively guide one's behavior and one's daily decisions for some period of time. Without such a guidepost, it is extremely difficult to have criteria that enable one to recognize when apparently small and rather insignificant decisions are, in fact, very important.

Goal Setting

The components of the investigative or preparatory step of career planning require thorough examination so as to enhance career planning. The first phase asks the question, "What is it I want to do?" To answer this, assess favorite tasks and the activities that bring personal reward. This will help identify *what* one would enjoy doing. In general, women tend to ask, "What skills do I have" or "What skills can I learn?" For women, answers to these questions are often further constrained by perceived external limitations. That is, women may limit a career goal because of the demands of a spouse or children; the demands or costs of child care; or the organizational require-ments of achieving managerial positions. In this early stage, women should not permit perceived demands or requirements to constrain their goal setting.

In order to set goals, several questions should be asked: "What types of managerial skills do I have or do I wish to develop? Are these managerial skills related to analytical, interpersonal, fiscal, or planning competencies? Do I wish to be the thinker or the fixer?" Questions related to job security and autonomy also should be answered. Lastly, ask questions such as: "How important is creativity to my career goals? Do I want to create my own service, product, or organization? Do I prefer maintenance activities or incremental change?"

Once a career goal identifies a management position as an objective, the second phase of goal setting addresses the questions of "*Where* do I want to do it?" More specifically, "In what setting do I want to use these skills?" and "In which areas do I need further training or knowledge?" Since human services covers an extremely broad range of types and structures of organizations, this phase includes many equally important questions. For any human service career, it is essential to understand the field of practice and client population for which one is best suited, to which one is the most committed, and which one finds the most enjoyable. Consequently, the first question to be answered is: "Is it more important for me (do I find it more enjoyable) to work with children, the aged, the disabled, or the terminally ill?" If the answer reveals no clear preference, then the next set of questions must be answered.

This second set of important questions is related to the type of agency in which one wishes to practice. Is there a preference for public, not-for-profit, or proprietary? A subset here might include the following questions: What are the distinctions with respect to current benefits, such as health, retirement, and so on? What are the distinctions between beginning and top salaries? Are there differences in the opportunities for advancement? What is needed to advance? How available are advancement opportunities?

Since the first stage of career planning involves setting long-range goals, it is important to understand how measurable and operational they must be in order to facilitate movement into management positions and later upward mobility.

The development of measurable goals means that one has to identify a plan that does more than state, "I want to have an important management position." Statements such as "I would like to be an executive director of a children's agency within five years" specify the level of the position, the type of agency desired, and the timeframe within which to achieve this goal.

Assessment

Once the goal has been established, one needs to move into the assessment phase. This means that one must have a knowledge of the skills, experience, education, and personal characteristics necessary for the position. It may take some data gathering to accumulate this information. One may need to read, talk with people in those positions or in similar positions, and spend time, if possible, following the daily activities of such professionals.

Given that routes to administrative positions in social work are varied and have changed over time, it is essential that one get data from a variety of sources, from a variety of settings, and from directors who vary in age, gender, professional and educational background, and in their career paths. This process may provide information that indicates routes may be different and yet equally successful; that paths may be different for men than for women; and that educational and experiential preparation may change over time.

The next assessment is a personal one. One must be able to objectively and realistically assess one's own current skills, talents, education, experience, and abilities to determine strengths and weaknesses. A comparison between those found to be important and/ or necessary and those currently possessed will provide the framework for the phase to follow.

Depending upon the "fit" of the comparison between current skills and talents and the skills and talents necessary for the career goal, it is essential to do reality testing. The individual must ask: "How realistic and achievable is the goal? Can I meet the timeframe I have established? To meet the goal within the timeframe, what other goals and values must be sacrificed? Must a relationship, children, recreation, or friends, be devalued, minimized, or postponed? What current earning might I have to give up while I pursue additional education or experience?" Given the answers to these questions, one must ask if the goal is motivating and meaningful enough in view of the short-term sacrifices to be made.

Once the information and personal assessment of the career goal are determined, one then needs to assess risk. Even after the collection of varied data, all informed decisions include an element of risk. What needs to be calculated is the amount of risk and the likelihood of failure.

Many career-planning experts suggest that one envision the "worst-case" scenario and review whether one could live with this outcome. For example, if to achieve the goal of becoming an executive director of a children's agency, one needs to obtain a graduate degree, which will reduce earnings for two to three years, a "worst-case" scenario might be: (1) not completing the degree; or (2) completing the degree and not being qualified for the position.

In order to reduce the risk, or minimize the potential for failure, one needs to assess what "fallback" positions would be available in the first case. With the additional education, but not the completion of a graduate degree, what positions would one be qualified for beyond the present competencies? Could one achieve interim certification and return to graduate education later? Could one switch educational fields and transfer credit? In the second case, might one be qualified for an executive director's position in an analogous agency, if not the one specified in the original goal? Would one be qualified for an associate director's position with the possibility of upward mobility?

If the "worst case" is unacceptable, it is probably a good idea to return to the first phase and reexamine one's career goals and gather additional information. Until the "fallback" position is a viable and tenable one, the individual should reassess matters. If the "worst case," or risk position, could not be tolerated (that is, one is temporarily unemployed or passed over for a promotion), then goals and strategies need to be reexamined. Throughout the process, it is important to remember that most decisions are not irrevocable. It is extremely freeing to understand that any decision can be changed, modified, or altered if the experience is different from that expected. In fact, with additional information, education, and learning, new information might present itself, which would suggest or mandate a reevaluation and, consequently, a change in decision. That is why career planning is lifelong.

Action Strategy

The third phase of goal setting raises the question, "How? How do I get the skills, education, and/or experience necessary for initial movement toward my career goal? Who can help me get there? Directly translated, this refers to finding a position that will use and polish existing skills or allow attainment of new skills. Identifying people and groups (such as mentors or networks) who will be significant to your progress is also important.

The action step to goal setting operationalizes the goal setting process. The action steps necessary to achieve the goal may include:

1. Skill attainment.
2. Additional experience.
3. Formal certification of skills or experience.
4. Professional contacts.

Consequently, the action steps should specify how to get the skills necessary if some are missing. The steps may include personal development through reading, formal training via continuing education or conference attendance, or the completion of a professional training or degree program.

If additional experience seems necessary, one may obtain that through volunteer experience, educational internships, or another position prior to the one desired. If experience and/or skills are already present, but not formally acknowledged, one may need to take an examination to certify the experience or skill or to develop a portfolio of completed assignments.

Another step is to identify the professional contacts useful or necessary to goal attainment. Actively looking for mentors and joining networks can be useful strategies so that one will know the "right person(s) at the right time."

CONCLUSION

In summary, career planning is a process that can be positively influenced by the seeker being an active agent, thereby increasing control of the situation. There are three phases of exploration:

1. Evaluating one's assets, desires, and values.
2. Determining areas of fit for step 1.
3. Considering where actual jobs exist related to areas in step 2. This is a useful approach to career planning for both sexes.

There are, however, continuing issues for women, which add a critical component to career planning. As noted in Chapter 2, for women the element of risk and the attendant behaviors associated with risk taking are often frightening. Women need to remind themselves constantly that successful people make mistakes and fail, and that they assess those mistakes and failures and learn from them. Women need to internalize the maxim that without risks, there are likely to be no grand successes. Other impediments to implementing goal setting involve women's proclivity to attempt to please everyone. If one has carefully assessed the impact of this career decision on one's environment and the significant others in it (spouse, friends, children, parents, colleagues), then one also should be able to predict some of the less-than-supportive behavior of these individuals as the plan becomes operational.

For women it may be necessary for some old, traditional patterns to change. One cannot continually say "yes" to everything and everyone if one is to pursue the goal within the timeframe. An exciting job opportunity that will provide immediate excitement and recognition, but will either deviate from one's career path or reduce the amount of time expended on goal-directed behavior probably should be turned down. The postponement of beginning a family, or the refusal to accept guilt because time has been reduced from family tasks, should have been examined, weighed, and balanced with the career planning decisions noted earlier.

In planning careers, women must first accept the reality of the issues involved in these patterns and choices and evaluate the costs and advantages of making the changes needed to survive and succeed. Then comes the task of managing the issues. To manage the issues means to develop skills in goal setting, planning, and problem solving, thereby translating insight into action designed for career advancement.

4 The Job Search

Bewildered, Marsha hangs up the telephone. She cannot believe what Craig has told her. When Craig, an executive director of another agency in the city, had been recruiting for an associate director, Marsha had telephoned him and recommended Sheila.

Now, Craig has telephoned, telling Marsha that he has hired someone else. In confidence, he told her why. He said that without Marsha's strong recommendation, he would not even have interviewed Sheila, because her resume was unimpressive. Furthermore, he said, Sheila interviewed poorly. She appeared to lack self-confidence and assurance in her ability to do the job. She also did not seem to know anything about the agency.

After thanking him for interviewing Sheila and for his telephone call, Marsha sits for a moment, wondering if Sheila had not really wanted the job or if she did not know how to pursue a new position. With these questions on her mind, she picks up the telephone, calls Sheila, and suggests that they have lunch next week. She also asks Sheila to bring her resume.

* * *

INTRODUCTION

Once career planning has taken place and the preparatory step completed, the job search process begins, either for the entry-level managerial position or the higher administrative post. In either case, in the first phase of this process one identifies the organization(s) to monitor so as to initiate a relationship or to apply for a position.

Throughout one's career, when one is in the phase of anticipating a career move, it is important to gather information as well as be prepared for action.

TARGETING THE ORGANIZATION

In the previous chapter, the career-planning analysis indicated that an assessment of the type, auspices, size, and location of the organization is important for goal setting. Once these are assessed, other aspects of the particular agency become invaluable for the job search.

Knowing what stage one is in enables one to maximize the "fit" between career goals, one's own career stage, and the organization's stages and needs. In order to have a clear picture of what a particular organization needs and the likely opportunities, challenges, and hazards for its employees, an organizational analysis is essential. Determining which of the following stages of organizational development the organization is in, will help suggest the potential fit or misfit relative to the individual's career stage.

These organizational stages are:

First phase: Origination and early development
Second phase: Growth through direction—beginning to establish policies.
Third phase: Growth through delegation—decentralizing.
Fourth phase: Growth through coordination—establishing controls over decentralized units.
Fifth phase: Growth through collaboration—maturity.

Clearly, in each phase of the organization's development, different skills are necessary because different functions are needed. For example, an agency in the early development phase probably has greater need for skills related to creativity and building and imaging the future. Likewise, the organizational manager needs to be an initiator, and must be comfortable with some ambiguity, flexibility, and perhaps, some instability.

If one's stage in career development—coupled with one's strengths—is in policy formulation and participatory decision making, an organization in phase two would be the "best fit." Conversely, if interorganization collaboration and coalition building, status, maturity, and predictability are essential, a more settled, mature, and well-established community organization ought to be targeted.

Strategically, these stages imply that perusing job listings in newspapers and professional publications is only one channel through which to find job opportunities and provides only part of the information about the agency. The informal channels of job information are often more important for management positions than the formal job announcements. Two such informal channels—mentoring and networking—will be discussed in detail in the following chapters.

PREPAIRING THE RESUME

The first task prior to submitting job applications is preparing the resume. While there are many points of view relative to the form, length, inclusion and exclusion of information, and style of the resume, there are some commonly agreed-on elements.

In addition to the cover letter, the resume is your introduction to the potential employer and should present the essential and outstanding elements of who you are relative to the position applied for. Even if you have carefully progressed through the career-planning and skill-acquisition steps, similar jobs may still require a slightly different mix of skills, experiences, and education. Consequently, it is important to prepare a "generic" resume that can be modified to fit different positions.

The "generic" resume should include the following:

Identifying Information	Full professional name, address, and telephone number
Formal Education	Degrees earned, institutions, dates, specializations
Paid, Related Experience	Title of positions, organizations, dates employed
Accomplishments	Programs initiated, grants received, articles published, conference speeches
Honors Received	Educational, employment, civic
Related Experiences	Paid, outside the field, volunteer, within the field
References	

To expand on this format in terms of identifying information, women should think about a professional name. Questions about the use of nicknames, initials, or married surname should be thought about in advance. Contact information should only be given for the business hours. Make it easy for the prospective employer to contact you.

If degrees or specializations require explanation, provide a brief statement. Similarly, if a formal job title inaccurately portrays the actual responsibilities and skills, describe these succinctly.

It should be noted that several items are omitted from the model resume, most notably demographic information. Birth date, marital status, and family responsibility are not required and might provide bias if presented. Women should be discouraged from including this information. Clearly, dates of degrees earned might provide information relative to age, just as gaps in an employment record might imply child-caring periods.

A list of references may be attached, or a note made that references will be provided upon request. One should be prepared with a varied list of past and current employers, professors, and professional colleagues.

In preparing the resume, one must decide how to format information— by chronological order (reverse or regular) or by functional areas. The former format is more common; the latter stresses skill areas more. One should remember that order, underlining, or the amount of space devoted to an area denotes emphasis to the reader.

The last suggestions are commonsense, but important. Proofread carefully. Typographical errors not only suggest that you are careless, but also may result in misinformation or inappropriate information. The resume should be easy to follow, relatively brief, and organized with headings that allow the reader to jump to the most important sections.

The basic resume should be short and easy to follow, and should provide the most salient information. If prepared on a word processor, customization of the resume is easy and quick. In this way, if one job stresses planning tasks, one can easily reorganize the material to highlight the skills and experiences most worthwhile. Likewise, if expertise with children is required, one can expand on the appropriate activities.

LETTER OF APPLICATION

Equally important to the resume is the letter of application. This allows one to customize the application to the particular agency, position, location, and so forth, irrespective of whether the resume is a generic or customized one. It also allows one to expand on the important aspects and explain in narrative fashion what otherwise might be difficult to understand from the resume.

The first paragraph of the letter should include the name of the position and how you learned about it and it should briefly present an idea of what you have to offer. The second paragraph should highlight your qualifications relative to the specifics of the position and explain your interest in this organization or type of work. It is appropriate here to include where you are in your career and the information about building skills, wanting new challenges, or attaining a career goal.

The third paragraph, if necessary, should explain any idiosyncracies in the resume, or expand on any points not covered within the resume or within the other paragraphs. For example, if there are blocks of time unaccounted for on the resume and you feel an explanation is in order or would enhance your opportunity to be interviewed, insert that information here. If you are changing careers, entering a career late due to family decisions or responsibilities, had an unexpected interruption in the education or career path due to personal illness or injury, an explanation may prevent the employer from second guessing.

The last paragraph should request an interview and provide contact information, including, if possible, available times and places for an interview. In all, the letter should be direct, brief, and upbeat.

LETTER TO REFEREE

A cardinal rule is to always ask the potential referees first before giving their name to a future employer. If you had their approval in the past, but several years have elapsed, it is advisable to recontact them and provide them with updated information about you as well as obtain updated information about them. If they have left the position, the field of practice, or died, your future employer will be unimpressed with your lack of knowledge of these important changes.

Whether you write to them or telephone to update and obtain permission, your opening remarks should clearly identify who you are, how they know you, and why you are contacting them. Do not be coy and pretend that you are just calling to catch up and then, unimportantly, say if you need a reference would they be willing to be one. Also, do not assume they remember you and the specifics. Provide that information. For example, you might say, "I hope that you remember me. I worked for you as a program director in 19— and initiated the collaborative program with agency X." Provide the referee with updated information about you (send them a current resume), a clear delineation of the position(s) to which you have applied, and any specifics about what you would like them to focus on: your analytical skills, interpersonal skills, your ability to balance multiple tasks, or your initiative.

In closing, repeat what you will send and what you are expecting them to do, the timeframe in which they have to complete it, and your thanks.

THE INTERVIEW

First impressions, whether directly related to a job or not, are human and are used by interviewers. Most employers seeking potential managers look for personality characteristics such as:

is energetic and vital
is confident and calm
speaks clearly and articulately
answers in detail
understands questions
appears responsible
is appropriately dressed

For women, these prescriptions may be filled with more uncertainty than for men. As will be discussed in later chapters, communication styles differ for men and women: What women may deliver as confident speech, may be received as overly aggressive. What may be delivered as enthusiasm, may be received as flightiness. What the employer considers appropriate dress for a man, may be considered "too masculine" for a woman. Thinking about a wardrobe for interviewing is not silly, but extremely practical. Wardrobe should include the consideration of a briefcase or portfolio. Papers falling out of one's arms or purse do not provide a professional and organized impression.

Be prepared for customary questions such as:

tell me about yourself
why should we hire you?
how long do you intend to stay with us?
how much money should you be earning?
why do you want to leave your current job?
what are your career goals?

Women must remember that it is okay to "sell oneself" during a job interview and not be shy about achievements and potential. Also, one should remember that these are not social questions or cocktail party conversation. Do not make your answers too short and do relate them to the job and to your skills. Several of these questions are delicate and should be answered honestly, but also in your best interest. For example, "How long do you intend to stay with us?" is probably best answered not in years, but with statements such as, "As long as challenges exist and advancement opportunities are provided." Likewise, if the question is worded, "How much are you currently making?" it is best to respond, "I'm worth $50,000."

Learn about the organization in advance by reading its brochures, by talking to its current or former employees, if possible, and by examining its budget and salary scale, if available. Know how large, how old, and how diversified the organization is. Learn something about its history and its current stature within the community. Also try to find out as much information about the opening and what is required as possible. Try to find out about advancement possibilities and requirements. Be prepared with your own questions. This shows preparation, interest, knowledge, and a clear idea of your potential within the organization. Ask about training programs, educational leave policy, fringe benefits package, and formal linkages to other organizations. It is important to remember that organizations want to maximize the fit between a new employee and the organization.

Women, more than men, need to be prepared to handle illegal questions such as: "Are you married? Does your husband plan to relocate with you? Do you have children? Do you plan to have children?" If you are unfortunate enough to be asked these questions, there are several ways to handle them. You can simply say that by law this question cannot be asked. You should realize that this may leave a negative impression. You can, alternatively, ask what relationship the question has to the job responsibilities or qualifications and then, depending on the response, indicate that it is an illegal question, or briefly provide the information, such as your arrangements for child care.

Or you can provide a succinct answer. "I have two children and I employ a part-time housekeeper." In any case, these are difficult questions to field and a pattern of response should be thought through in advance. The positive side is that the further up in management one moves, the less these questions are asked because the employer realizes that you have successfully dealt with these issues before.

Also, be prepared that the higher the position or the further you go in the interview process, there is the possibility for group interviews. A top-level manager may be interviewed first by the person to whom this position is accountable, but after that, interviews might be set up with groups of future subordinates, members of the policy-making body (a group from the board of directors, for example), or a peer group of program directors.

All of the previous suggestions apply to group interviewing sessions as well. However, as in any group process, try to include everyone in the group when you answer; try to allow as many individuals as possible to ask questions; try to draw out silent members; and be sensitive to being placed in the middle between vying organizational members.

JOB NEGOTIATION

When the position is offered, the important stage of negotiating the contract begins. Women, particularly women being solicited and hired into management positions, need to think about the array of areas around which there are negotiating possibilities (or discriminatory actions) beyond that of the initial salary. Also keep in mind that once the job is offered and within the timeframe specified, all negotiations and counter proposals are possible and that the job is yours until you turn it down.

Salary

The initial salary offered is quite likely from a range of salary possibilities and probably dependent on overt variables such as credentials, experience, and past earnings, although these variables work against women. Covert variables sometimes utilized are the earnings (or supposed earnings of a spouse), the notion of "cheap" labor, and the salary you may have suggested that you might take. It is important to keep in mind that the first salary offered is seldom the best that can be offered.

Although the initial salary is of immediate as well as long-term importance, it can be mitigated if merit salary and promotional opportunities are frequent and of significant proportion. Thus, biannual opportunities for evaluation, significant merit increments, and promotions may quickly make up for an initial salary somewhat lower than desired. Conversely, a higher initial salary with infrequent evaluative opportunities and miniscule merit increments will retard future earning potentials.

Less common in the human services, but not to be ignored, are the potentials for bonuses or incentive pay plans. Usually these do not get added to base salary and consequently, the effect of these dollar increases is not cumulative, they offer tangible incentives for performance. Pay incentives may be described related to the ability to retain a proportion of grants and contract monies attained for the organization.

Benefits

There are many benefits that can be seen and used as "trade-offs" or "add-ons" to the basic salary. Certainly, health care plans are the most widely used and understood as part of the benefits package. A close examination of the array of "covered" services includes dental, mental health, and long-term disability, which are preferred inclusions. The proportion of deductibles and percentage of reimbursement can make sizable differences in one's expendible income. The coverage of spouse and children ought to be examined.

Private, not-for-profit human service agencies tend not to have retirement programs. However, it may be possible to negotiate an annual amount to be placed into a private retirement program, which has the advantage of not counting as taxable income.

Expense accounts are as common for social work managers as they are for corporate executives. Finding out not only the dollar amount, but the discretionary ability to expend those dollars is important. For example, can the account cover expenses for liquor as well as for food? For fees to attend job-related luncheons and dinners? Fees for spouses to attend if that is expected? What are reimbursable travel expenses? Are there set per diem amounts or will the agency cover all real expenses?

Educational leave policy for both short-term workshops and conferences and longer-term educational leaves should be negotiated to the extent possible. Will tuition and per diem or travel expenses be paid for professional development?

A final set of fringe benefits, even less common than educational leave, but particularly important to women, involves the opportunities for flex time and child care. These can be offered either in the form of on-site availability or as items in the benefits package.

Support Staff

To do an effective job, the organization must provide necessary supports. The time to ensure that these supports will be available is during the initial negotiating phase of the new job or the promotion. Clearly, staff are of essential importance. One must ascertain whether clerical and technical staff exist in sufficient proportions to get the jobs completed. Similarly, are the professional staff adequate in number and training for current as well as future needs? What are the organizational opportunities and supports for these employees relative to on-the-job training and professional development? What budgetary and personnel latitude exists for the recruitment, promotion, and termination of employees?

Equipment also must be considered and evaluated for your own position as well as for the staff. Computers and adequate software, audiovisual aids, dictaphones and transcribers, photocopiers, and state-of-the-art telephones must be assessed.

Work Environment

Functional space is important, but so is the proximity to other important organizational members and functions. Also, as in the corporate sector, space and its usage denotes status, power, and authority.

Clearly, the space must be large enough to accommodate routine and expected tasks. So, if small group meetings are part of routine responsibility, an office with a large enough space for a small group to meet or an office with an adjoining meeting room is required. Pay attention to furnishings that may denote differential position within the hierarchy such as wooden versus metal furniture, carpeting, windows, office size, and office location. To what extent can you modify the environment through color choice, wall hangings, and so on? Will the organization pay for any of these?

Contract

The contract, itself, has some negotiable aspects, such as the length of time of the contract, the conditions for nonrenewal, and, sometimes, "buy-out" clauses. The latter may be important if the organization is, or has recently been, in major transition. Although buy-out clauses offer some protection from capricious board decisions, external situations could affect the organizational design or structure, precipitating a termination "without cause." Under such circumstances, legal as well as some fiscal protection may be advisable.

Once these concerns are negotiated, the contract should specify as many of these in writing as possible. If the organization utilizes a more standardized contract form that cannot accommodate some of the terms, request an additional letter that details the negotiated terms.

CONCLUSIONS

These prescriptions include strategies for women to overcome an array of overt as well as covert, conscious as well as unconscious sets of organizational barriers.

Further, they are often the "informal" advice that a male mentor passes on to his male protege. Excluded from this advice, women often move up in spite of poor resumes or incomplete negotiating processes.

5 Mentoring

Sheila watches her office door close as she sits shaking her head and wondering what more can happen. The employee who has just left is angry about a decision Sheila made and has decided to file a grievance against her. She has always had problems with him.

Sheila's mind then turns to other problems. The director wants a revision of the budget; a new program is possible if only she can complete the proposal for a sizable grant in time; and correspondence and phone calls have piled up, because she has attended so many meetings to discuss the long-range planning the board of directors is undertaking. This is not the first time she has faced a situation of having a lot to do without knowing how to prioritize.

She sits back in her chair, wondering how Jan would handle the situation. Jan is the division director of the Area Agency on Aging in the city. The division is three times the size of Sheila's and Sheila has often talked with Jan about job-related issues. Moreover, Jan taught Sheila some of the skills she now uses. Jan also has served as a sounding board for problems, and Sheila has felt comfortable enough with Jan to reveal her fears, worries, or concerns about job-related situations. While they are not really friends, their relationship—combination of teacher-colleague-and-supporter—is special. It occurs to Sheila that theirs may be considered a mentoring type of relationship. With a big sigh, Sheila admits to herself, "I really could use some help to clarify my thinking about this situation." She then picks up the phone and calls Jan.

* * *

INTRODUCTION

Mentoring as a concept and as a strategy is of dynamic and current relevancy to all women, and should be particularly so for women in social work. It is integral to overcoming internal and external barriers and central to the concepts of career development and networking. Often these terms are familiar, but their meaning is vague. Given how few women are in social work administrative positions, those currently aspiring to these positions must utilize all the support they can get.

There is something blatantly hypocritical in any system that professes to deliver humanitarian services to the public, to exorcise discrimination, injustice, and inequality in all aspects of life, and to promote progress and "the pursuit of happiness" while in actuality it perpetuates the worst kinds of discrimination through insensitivity and a blind adherence to society's status quo. However necessary mentoring may be for the success of women in other lines of work, it is of critical importance to a female student of social work and to her employment future. Mentoring and networking are the main source of power women have in this or any other field. Yet the increased enrollment of part-time social work students decreases sustained contact with faculty, making it difficult, if not impossible, for working students to seek mentors among their educators (Taibbi, 1983; Stafford, 1987; York, Henley, & Gamble, 1988).

Although mentoring and networking are two different systems by which women can experience emotional and career growth, advancement, ongoing education, and success in the field, the two can be closely related. Today's mentor may become tomorrow's network associate and vice versa. The two functions are being given more and more attention by women. "Old boys' networks" are being examined and understood for what they potentially provide. Women are setting up their own networks or finding ways to be included in men's networks through the use of their mentors, professors, or older family members.

With the growing awareness of the value of mentoring, women are no longer waiting to be "discovered" (McLane, 1980, p. 156). They are actively seeking out mentors who can give them career guidance, advice, and support. This means they must learn to overcome a lifetime of social conditioning that regards using another person for one's own advancement as immoral, regards assertiveness as unfeminine, and the mixing of business with social functions as impolite (Stern, 1981). At the same time, many women are bringing feminine traits of sharing, caring, and support to the workplace, even while adopting male success methodology. It may prove to be a most happy blend (Levinson, 1978).

In recent years attention has been given to formal rules and practices that lead to a gender-segregated educational and professional system. More difficult to detect and prove but equally as powerful are the informal norms and practices that generate sex discrimination and differential advantage. Another direct relationship between mentors and networks is the central position a mentor commands in the "male homosocial network" (Lipman-Blumen, 1984). The mentor protects and shapes his protege's progression throughout the college years and beyond. The mentor acts as a kind of "gatekeeper" to important positions within the college or professional school system and in the nonacademic world. Few women have been included in this network or mentored, as evidenced in the unsuccessful tenure battles by female faculty members in the 1970s and by the absence of dramatic change in the social work management statistics by gender (Corcoran, Robbins, Hepler, & Magner, 1987).

As indicated earlier, these gatekeeping or supportive roles apparently begin as early as graduate education and may cause female students to choose the administrative track less frequently than their male peers. Unfortunately, the differential that exists in mentoring opportunities continues in social work employment.

DEFINITIONS

Many differing definitions of mentoring seem to exist. The consensus is that it is more than supervision. Mentoring may be defined as "an expansion in depth and commitment of the supervisory role beyond supportive, administrative, and teaching functions. It entails more than carrying out tasks, developing a working relationship: mentorship requires the active participation of both parties and their agreement that the relationship will address the development needs of both" (Taibbi, 1983, p. 237; Merriam, 1983).

Interestingly, in the Dictionary of Occupational Titles, mentoring is rated as the highest order people-related skill and is described in terms of employee actions: "Deals with individuals in terms of their overall life adjustment behavior in order to advise, counsel, and/or guide them with regard to problems that may be resolved by legal, scientific, clinical, spiritual and/or other professional principles" (1977, p. 1370).

Although many terms such as coach, guide, teacher, counselor, and godfather have been used, recent research suggests that these words really represent different kinds of supportive relationships that exist on a continuum of power (Missirian, 1982). While a mentor can assume any one or all of the less powerful roles, the reverse is not true. The other roles do not have the degree of influence or power that mentors have on their proteges. Typically, the emotional involvement in a true mentoring relationship goes far beyond the utility of the relationship in terms of sponsorship or career modeling.

That is to say, mentor-protege relationships appear to differ from role-modeling relationships in that mentoring takes on the element of teaching and coaching (Kanter, 1975; Collins, 1983, pp. 1–10) designed to "promote" or enable a "lesser ranked" person to advance within a chosen system. Role modeling or teaching is more passive and is a less interrelated relationship in which one can be admired and emulated from a social, physical, and emotional distance.

On the other hand, the mentor-protege relationship is one in which each partner becomes vulnerable to the other. It is this willingness to be vulnerable that is the key to the issue of trust, which in turn is the key to the development of a true mentoring relationship. Consequently, the fundamental distinction between the relationships of teacher, sponsor, and coach is one of emotional involvement (Merriam, 1983).

A mentoring relationship provides the chance to promote the career development and psychosocial development of both individuals. A mentor can coach, protect, and give exposure, visibility, and challenging work assignments to a protege in order to teach the "ropes" of organizational life and to prepare the protege for advancement. The mentor provides role modeling, acceptance and confirmation, and advice for the purpose of helping the protege develop a sense of competence, effectiveness, and efficiency in the managerial role. In turn, the mentor receives respect and recognition from peers as well as affirmation and approval from the protege (Kram, 1983).

Thus, a mentor is not just a friend, nor is a mentor constantly on call to vent emotions, grievances, and frustrations. Unfortunate as it may seem, mentors, particularly good ones, are not exclusively yours—they often are mentoring others. It is also important to remember constantly that mentors are not peers. While peers may be an important part of networking, they are not mentors.

ELEMENTS OF THE MENTORING RELATIONSHIP

What the above definition and scenario should suggest is that mentoring is a key strategy for upward mobility for both men and women, but it is likely to be even more important for women given their socialization and organizational realities (York, Henley, & Gamble, 1988). Subtle and sometimes unnoticed barriers exist for competent, capable women because they are not given proper childhood and adult preparation, coaching, or training in order to be fully competitive in today's management world. The key to success for women is to understand the "game of working" and that success is more achievable for women when they have a mentor who is senior and capable of providing support, introductions, and access to needs (Collins, 1983; Harragan, 1984).

The literature notes that most leaders have been selected to assume their roles via a complex protege system. Not only is education, training, and technical knowledge necessary, but also "secret know-how"—the special knowledge and skills a protege observes in the "pro." Because the two create a dyadic leader-follower relationship, women may not be chosen for this special attention because they seldom proclaim their worth, do not actively seek a mentor, and fear that it may be perceived as a sexual relationship if the mentor is male (Gerrard, Oliver, & Williams, 1976; Kram, 1985). Studies report (McLane, 1980) that two of every three senior executives who had a mentor, earned more money, were happier with their career progress, and found greater pleasure in their work.

The double-bind for female managers is the disassociation with both male and female employees. A female manager is cut off from women because of her rank and from men because of her sex. Consequently, she needs the support of a mentor for psychological as well as for career reasons. Women aware of their minority status are often afraid to aid others because they may be perceived as organizers of future trouble (McLane, 1980). Some who made it to the top with little help along the way feel that women in lower level jobs should have to make it on their own, as well. Much of the literature supports the premise that women who succeed usually report that at least one of their male superiors was instrumental in helping them. Usually the man selects the woman from a group of her peers and teachers her about the "most political responses to be made in her new situation." His patronage protects her from those who do not want her to join their upper ranks. If her mentor moves up the organizational ladder, she moves up also.

The quickest access to a higher position is through direct contact with the mentor (Larwood & Wood, 1977; Smith & Grenier, 1982; Riley & Wrench, 1985). The old boys' network is usually the first to know about a future job opening, and news of it is spread informally and quickly through casual conversation, often in a social setting. In this way, the better positions are filled long before any formal notice of the vacancy is publicized.

Women must rid themselves of the notion that good work, reliability, and organizational loyalty are the most essential elements to upward mobility. These are quite obviously necessary, but not sufficient, conditions for upward mobility.

Mentoring is "one of the most complex and developmentally important relationships a man can have in early adulthood" (Levinson, 1978, pp. 97–101). It is a relationship perhaps even more critical for a woman than for a man. While mentoring is usually done in the workplace, it also can be done

by a friend, neighbor, or spouse. The mentor's crucial function is as support-
er and facilitator of the protege's goals and ambitions.

There would appear to be fairly substantial evidence for the importance
and virtues of being a protege. There are, however, concomitant responsibilities with being a protege. Close contact and exchange are characteristics of
a mentoring relationship that often result in the sharing of the personal
and professional thoughts and aspirations of both parties. The protege
should take caution not to breach any confidence of trust by revealing issues that would place the mentor in a vulnerable position. As a courtesy
and a way of staying current in the relationship, the protege should also
keep the mentor informed of his or her implementation of ideas they have
exchanged.

The benefits to mentors should also not be overlooked. It is in their best
interest to promote people who share their ideas and who are loyal to them.
Proteges can also enhance a mentor's position in others' eyes by verbalizing
support of actions and abilities (Collins, 1983). Furthermore, professionals of
higher status usually derive pleasure in "passing on" their ideas to an
up-and-coming professional. This aspect of the relationship can be stimulating to the mentor and assist him or her in remaining on the cutting edge of a
chosen profession through frequent and intense exchange of ideas. Furthermore, it is esteem-enhancing to be respected by and to act as a reference for
a protege.

SELECTING A MENTOR

Having a mentor who can teach, support, advise, critique, and provide
opportunities is relevant to a woman at *all* stages of her career. The literature
also suggests that a woman choose someone who is her senior in experience
and power. This mentor can be called many things such as teacher or
sponsor, but she should be a "winner" (Jardin, 1977, pp. 41, 162). In
realizing the importance of mentoring to career development, women
should be cautious and contemplative when selecting a mentor. This is
advised even though many mentoring relationships evolve gradually out of
shared interests and styles and mutual professional respect rather than as a
result of the planful efforts of either party.

Women should be more directed and assertive about their involvement
in mentoring relationships; essential to such an endeavor is their self-
knowledge of what needs development (Collins, 1983). From this self-
knowledge, women can develop general goals and awarenesses that make
choosing a mentor a more relaxed endeavor. These awarenesses may likely
yield a more successful "match" of mentor and protege.

Criteria that should be considered in the selection of a mentor include:

possesses a rank higher up in the organizational ladder
is an authority in his or her field
is influential (possesses sanctioned power)
is interested in the growth and development of the protege
shows a willingness to commit time and emotion to the relationship
    (Collins, 1983).

Mentors are extremely valuable and are able to provide assistance to
their proteges in a number of pragmatic ways. These include the following:

teaches by example
imparts valuable "inside" information that otherwise is unavailable to
    persons of your status
provides feedback on your progress and others' perceptions of you
shares your dreams and encourages you
provides counsel, advice, and support
introduces you to the corporate structure, its politics and its players
expands your vision and encourages you to "think big" and see a "bigger
    picture"
boosts self-esteem by believing in you and by providing his or her
    "stamp of approval"
provides upward mobility within your organization or field (Collins,
    1983, pp. 22–28)

At this point, it is important to more fully describe the behaviors and
roles of the mentor. While the role of "teaching by example" might also fit a
sponsor, coach, teacher, the relationship ought to be close enough to encourage questioning and reactions in an open and honest manner about that
teaching. Imparting valuable information should include the provision of
information such as:

Where does the power in the organization truly lie?
What are the organizational standards, norms, values, heroes, ideology,
    and history?
What are the paths to advancement as well as the blind alleys?
What are the skills and competencies needed to succeed and advance?
What are the acceptable modes of visibility?
What are the characteristic stumbling blocks and patterns of failure?
    (Machlowitz, 1978, p. 166).

These attributes may not all be present in a single mentor. Therefore, a
woman may choose to be involved with more than one mentor simultaneously.

The invaluable assessments that a mentor can provide relative to your progress and to how others view you cannot be underestimated. People can change and modify their styles of work, their interpersonal dynamics, their dress, and voice tone and modulation, if they find any of these to be obstructions to advancement and if it is reasonable to do so. Having someone assess not only the soundness of your ideas, but whether they are plausible within the organizational and/or professional politics is of paramount importance.

Additionally, a mentor can provide that subtle evaluative information usually not asked for, nor given, in routine organizational annual reviews. For example, an evaluation might conclude that your work performance and productivity are "above average," but your boss may have shared a sense that you do not take the initiative often enough.

To the extent that one can truly share one's professional dreams and aspirations with a mentor, the mentoring relationship allows legitimate expression with someone who will not find your goals a threat or a conflict of interest (which is why the mentor cannot be your boss). The honest and unembarrassed sharing of these dreams allows the protege to frame plans for achieving goals as well as to help enlarge and expand those dreams when they seem too limited and limiting. Having someone whom you believe in, who is successful, and believes in you, is the support necessary to move through the passages of professional development. When the normal doubts arise—such as, "Can I really perform at the next level? Do I have the requisite skills to handle that job?"—external validation of worth will make the difference.

Sponsorship through introductions to the "right" people, through invitations to the inside functions, and through promoting your talents and abilities are additional benefits for fast tracking. Eventually, talented and motivated employees get the introductions and invitations, but the earlier this occurs in one's career, the earlier the possibilities for advancement. While women can learn to be more self-promotional, it is also easy for them to be differentially labeled as "pushy."

Gender Issues in Mentoring

Upon reviewing the criteria for selection of a mentor, one can conclude there are more men than women who meet the requirements. Clearly, there are more male mentors because there are more men than women at the top of organizations and in possession of more power, even in the social work field (Josefowitz, 1980, p. 97). Furthermore, until very recently, those few women who rose in their field have usually done so with little assistance from others. Some of the literature suggests these women are "Queen Bees," who are unwilling to help any younger women because of feelings of jealousy and fear and the belief that independent struggle builds character (Collins, 1983, pp. 107–108; Josefowitz, 1980, pp. 97–99).

Interestingly enough, there is support on both sides for choices of same-gender or cross-gender mentors. Men can provide information and access to gamesmanship understanding as well as to power itself (Harragan, 1984; Collins, 1983). Others suggest that same-gender mentors are more desirable for women because only another woman can fully understand the plight, promise, and hope of other women's professional journeys (Welch, 1980; Clawson & Kram, 1984; Fitt & Newton, 1981). One woman author capsulizes some of the dilemmas by indicating that women mentors know from experience, but male mentors are more powerful (McLane, 1980).

Since any mentoring relationship requires that so much time be invested together and is so emotionally intense, proteges in cross-gender mentoring relationships may be vulnerable to dangerous gossip and sexual innuendos. Such suggestions could lead to career damage for the woman in a cross-gender mentoring relationship (Machlowitz, 1978).

It is probably undeniable that successful women had to try harder than their male counterparts. In their struggle to grow and advance, they have acquired reservoirs of knowledge which, if shared, would be valuable to other women. These women should not forget there are others in the process of achieving. These women should be challenged to feel an obligation and desire to mentor younger women and women who enter the job market late (Josefowitz, 1980). It should be understood that it is difficult for women to function as mentors given the stresses of a world dominated by men. Thus, the cycle continues. With few women in powerful positions, the stresses are increased. With increased stress, there is a potential reduction in the interest and time to mentor a woman. Consequently, if women are mentored at all, it will more likely continue to be by men.

However, when the mentor is male and the protege female, the man may regard her as attractive but not managerial, as intelligent but an impersonal "pseudo-male," or as a charming little girl who cannot be taken seriously. In short, there may be a tendency for a male mentor to make the female less than she is and often the woman accepts this.

In all likelihood, the greater the resolution of a man's masculine and feminine components, the better able he is to be a mentor for a woman. This resolution phase usually occurs at mid-life when a man no longer projects his feminine qualities like nurturing, fostering, inspiring, and tenderness onto women, but accepts them in himself and uses them to further someone else's career. Consequently, it is at this point that men can best mentor women. In earlier adulthood, the idea of a nonromantic relationship with a woman is difficult for many men to imagine, and if a younger man does attempt a mentoring relationship with a woman, he tends to make her "think like a man," which distorts her personal development by emphasizing her intelligence, talent, and ambition but excluding her femininity with its softer qualities. This leaves her with masculine strengths but also with masculine limitations.

Thus, the conclusion is that the most successful mentorship occurs between a female protege and a male mentor when he is six to eight years older than she, but not until the male has reached his mid-forties, when he is able to regard his female protege as a capable adult, not just as a charming "girl." The emergence of growing numbers of "older women" into graduate schools and the workplace may tend to skew this orderly pattern of development. This trend is of particular significance to professional social work careers, because it would appear that older women are not likely candidates for mentoring. The notion that older people are passed over for management training because age plays a significant part in the selection process is well documented (Basil, 1972; Josefowitz, 1980).

LIFE CYCLE OF MENTORING

"Looking for one person to carry you throughout your career can lead to chronic disappointment" (Machlowitz, 1978, p. 165). The suggestion that a particular mentoring relationship will not last a lifetime is reinforced by a number of authors (Josefowitz, 1980). We know, especially in the profession of social work, that all people grow and change, and that as they do so, their needs likewise change. These personal and professional evolutions may soon find the current mentoring relationship oppressive or unfulfilling. One person or both may feel compelled to either sever the mentoring relationship or to attempt to transform it into a collegial friendship. Josefowitz (1980) cautions proteges to note that some mentoring relationships end in bitterness. Awareness of both parties' needs, and especially the needs that the mentoring role provides the mentor, may assist both in sensitively parting company.

The mentor is not a parent substitute; his part in the protege's development is "transitory." He must be a mixture of both parent and peer in equally balanced proportions. Eventually the protege may gain knowledge and experience that surpasses the mentor's, the protege becomes a mentor herself or himself, and the older mentor becomes a part of the original protege's network of peers.

The other side of choosing a mentor is ending a mentoring relationship so one can move on to learn different and new skills, experience new organizational patterns, and form new, expanded networks. Consequently, knowing when and how to end the mentoring relationship is extremely important. After the protege "outgrows" his mentor, there can be an awkward period of conflict and bad feelings on both sides (unless the termination is due to involuntary factors). Often the value of the relationship is not fully recognized until long after its termination. It is at this point that the protege's personality is enhanced by making the mentor a part of herself or himself, by internalizing all that the mentor has passed on to the protege.

The mature mentoring personality will also recognize the protege's "coming of age" and may even assist the protege in assessing the point at which the apprenticeship should end. Women should be careful to guard against an overdependency on a male mentor, as they have been socialized from childhood into such a dependency pattern (Collins, 1983).

Lastly, because there are a variety of needs to be met in a mentoring relationship it is not always possible to find a single person to be responsive to them all. Some persons may choose to become involved in several mentoring relationships. One should be cautious in doing so, as such relationships are intense and deserve the protege's commitment and consistency in their maintenance. The protege should be aware of his or her ability and energy level in maintaining multiple relationships.

CONCLUSIONS

With awareness of the need for support, information sharing, and social contact also comes awareness that a woman has difficulty finding female mentors when she is high on the management ladder. Women in high administrative positions seeking top-level mentors will be limited, in the majority of cases, to men as advisors. This problem will eventually lessen as more women learn to identify and befriend key people in their organizations, establish networks, and reach executive positions.

Ideally the male managers of today who are mentoring females also should be actively training them to be mentors themselves. This would have the effect of generating "affirmative action," not only by the male mentor but also by his female protege, to seek out other proteges and thus discover those women who do not yet have the courage to seek support on their own. It would also encourage the "Queen Bees" who have moved above the crowd and no longer feel any commitment, responsibility, or compassion for the women still struggling below, to recognize that paying dues pays off (Larwood & Wood, 1977). Mentoring is a reciprocal system. The protege learns, but in turn, teaches the mentor and provides a support service.

6 Networking

Joe stops Sheila in the hall and asks if she is planning to attend the Mayor's annual Christmas open house. Sheila answers that she does not know if she can afford to take the time to attend the affair. Joe states as he walks away, "It will be an excellent networking opportunity."

Sheila thinks about networking as she walks back to her office. She has never totally understood the concept and has often thought about it as a professional word for friendship. However, it is indeed intriguing to meet important people and try to establish relationships and, she has to admit, there are times when people whom she has met out of the office have helped her to advance her career and improve her work performance.

She is puzzled because many times, networking seems too exclusive, as though one were trying to be better than other people and ignoring the "less important people" for the more prestigious individuals. She remembers a long conversation she had with Jan about the importance of networking. Jan encouraged Sheila to meet individuals specifically who could be an advantage to her in the present or the future. Jan tried to indicate how networking differs from mentoring. She said that networking is more collegial and involves numerous individuals, but is not as in-depth or as personal as a mentoring relationship.

Sheila smiles as she remembers being at the Mayor's Volunteer Award luncheon earlier this year and meeting the county treasurer. That meeting seemed serendipitous, when four days later she was able to call on him to break a deadlock concerning a funding proposal she had submitted to the county office. She remembers realizing she had felt that the two hours spent at the event had paid off.

With that recollection, Sheila puts away her work and leaves for the Mayor's Christmas open house.

* * *

INTRODUCTION

Although mentoring and networking are two different strategies by which women in management or aspiring to management can experience personal and career growth, advancement, ongoing education, and success in the field, the two are closely related. Today's mentor may become tomorrow's network associate and vice versa.

The two functions are being given more and more attention by women in the workplace and women in management in particular. "Old boys' networks" also are being examined and understood for what they potentially provide (Kerson & Alexander, 1979; Brass, 1985). Women are setting up their own networks or finding ways to be included in the men's networks through the use of their mentors, bosses, or family members.

Sometimes networking is viewed by some as a selfish move since it is not seen as benefiting the organization or the family. Indeed, networking does involve women getting together to benefit themselves directly in the workplace and only indirectly to benefit their husbands, children, parents, companies, communities, or any of the many "others" they have been socialized to support or to place first. Networking is women's way of doing something for themselves. It is women saying, "I want more. I want more money. I want more responsibility. I want more fulfillment from my work. I want more power."

However, the unselfish part of networking involves women getting together not only to say, "I want," but also women saying, "I want to give. I want to help. I want to share." Ultimately, networking has a dual focus: (1) what can others do for me? and (2) how can I give to and help other women?

Clearly, in the process of gaining jobs, favors, or access to power, and information the basic principle of networking is, "Who do you know?" While it would seem that this is a relatively easy principle to apply, women find it difficult to create or join a network even though they know that benefits are derived from it and that limited access and slower mobility occur without it (Tickamyer & Bokemeier, 1984; York, Henley, & Gamble, 1985).

DEFINITIONS

Networking is a concept, a technique, and a process. "As a concept, it can change your whole way of thinking about what it takes to succeed in business. As a technique, it will introduce you to stimulating, knowledgeable allies you did not know you had. As a process, it knows no limits—and neither will you if you use it to its fullest potential" (Welch, 1980).

Networking is an investment; the more you invest, the more rewards you can reap. The areas in which one can reap these benefits are in "visibility, familiarity, and image" (Smith, 1983, p. 52). One can attain visibility and familiarity simply by being involved in the network.

In addition to the positive aspects of networking relative to resources and information, the following functions are equally important:

a different point of view and objective feedback
social contacts
humor (jokes, "war stories")
resources
confidantes
an acceptable outlet for anger
sympathy
a source of praise and reassurances (Witkin-Lanoil, 1984, p. 132).

Given that a woman manager often leads an isolated existence, that her style may be perceived as weak or certainly as different, or that she may be excluded from the work group, a woman's network can be a substantiating, validating experience through which she can hear different points of view or hear comparable experiences and frustrations voiced. It should be a place where praise and reassurance are more readily given since these are not colleagues and because other women may value the same outcomes as well as share the same leadership styles. Further, it may provide objective feedback as a consequence, free from direct competitiveness or from gender-biased experience.

The components that the network may provide relating to confidantes, release for anger, and a place for humor, or the sharing of "war stories" is vital to the mental health of any organizational employee. Many people cannot and, indeed, should not, vent their anger at other employees, at bosses, or at the organizational environment directly. But if not displaced at all, this anger builds, becoming dysfunctional for the individual. It may be associated with anxiety, depression, or substance abuse in the individual, or with poor work performance, absenteeism, or high turnover in the organization. Humor is another healthy mechanism for coping with the inequities and frustrations of organizational life, discrimination, and sexism. While not structural solutions to these problems, the functions can reduce the unhealthy notions that women otherwise have that their behaviors are responsible for the prejudices held by their colleagues, superiors, and subordinates (Stern, 1981).

So, while the more tangible outcomes of networking may be upward mobility, increased information, and contacts, the functions outlined here are essential to the development of self-confidence and the continuance of healthy responses to organizational issues. Although some information and experience cannot or should not be shared with colleagues on the job, men do have more built in on-the-job opportunities to share some of these issues than do women managers, who are often isolated.

Consequently, networks are composed of diverse women, some of whom have already achieved and some who are desirous of achieving. Women already in high-level positions obtain satisfaction in networks from the supportive functions and, perhaps, from potential opportunities to find proteges. Conversely, women not yet high in an organizational hierarchy may benefit from the access to information and power as well as from potential opportunities to find mentors.

Thus, networking is a way of filling the void that isolated women in managerial positions find. Because there are still few women at the top, not only are they isolated, but their career patterns may be somewhat idiosyncratic. But their unique circumstance need not doom the woman manager to isolation. The fact that many successful women are bombarded with female envy as well as by male hostility means that she needs women like herself even more.

Consequently, networking becomes essential therapy as a way for coping. Networks help women cope with a complex blend of career achievements, organizational realities, and personal life. There is no reason why the successful career woman has to be a lonely tower of strength or a standard-bearer for all women. Indeed, it may be a measure of a successful woman's strength that she can reach out to others, ask for sharing, and request help. Another benefit of networking is the prevention of professional burnout. One study found that the attitudes of co-workers strongly influenced the quality of new professionals' experiences. Weak supervision might be compensated for by co-workers who were available and sympathetic (Kravetz & Austin, 1984). However, this kind of collegial support is often unavailable so that isolation and loneliness become key factors in precipitating burnout.

Communication patterns within organizations demonstrate that employees prefer to (1) talk with others whom they perceive as helpful to their organizational development; (2) communicate with those who can make them feel more secure; and (3) communicate to improve their power and status within the organization (Jackson, 1969; Mintzberg, 1973). It is not surprising then that men tend to communicate with other men and ignore women because they do not perceive women as being of help in making them powerful, improving their status, or making them feel more secure.

The elitist nature of networks is often uncomfortable for women. Most women in networks are those who are or want to be at or near the top in their careers; they are women of success and orientation, with ambition and career motivation. Yet, women may still feel uncomfortable with the exclusion from these functions of other women, such as support staff and subordinates.

The desire to form networks indicates a desire to tap into other women as resources. The reason that these groups have created some backlash from other women as well as from men is that they are composed of women who are not afraid to label themselves as elite and are not afraid to apply words like ambition, power, prestige, and status to their desires. Women who have climbed to the top and who see the process of career achievement as desirable and necessary, want to make contact with one another. That is the central idea behind networks.

Women breaking new ground and filling positions historically and traditionally held by men may well encounter everything from suspicion to obstruction to defiance and, only rarely, support. It is difficult to experience these attitudes from business colleagues without the potential of turning these attitudes into explanations of one's own inadequate performance or ineffective style. By sharing "war stories" with or describing experiences to other women in like situations, one can gain a better perspective and reduce self-criticism and blame.

DEVELOPING A NETWORK

Networks can take both the formal as well as the informal structure. Formally, they exist as ongoing support groups and professional women's associations. Informally, they consist of opportunities to have business breakfasts, lunches, or dinners; engage in sports; or attend functions—such as Sheila does in the chapter's introduction—at which opportunities will exist to reach out to new and different groups of people. Networks can also exist, or be created, within or outside one's workplace. Each has its own set of benefits as well as difficulties.

For example, within one's own organization, the process of beginning a network is more simple, at least from the standpoint of identification and communication. The single most important point is to interact with similarly situated persons. Managerial women should network with other managerial women, not with supervisors or with secretaries. Be prepared for some possible adverse reaction within the organization to a group of women socializing together. To enhance organizational support, networks within organizations should function in an open and a visible fashion. One overt way to do this is to request the use of the board room for meetings.

Reaching out to create a network outside the work group, within one's own professional organization, creates different problems. Here the initiation must fall to one individual or to a small group of women who will choose a date, place, and time and insert an announcement in the professional newsletter. The ongoing agenda may be based on who attends and for what purposes. Because these women may know each other less well and work in different organizational settings, the reaching out to each other may take a longer time period.

Since networks may not exist that fit the woman manager's need, or they may exist in places or at times that are prohibitive, she may be required to establish her own network. Lunch is a key element and choice for networking. Male executives have luncheon meetings (quite often paid for by the organization), while many female executives eat alone, either at their desks or out. Not only should lunch be used for a change of pace, but it is an opportunity to network on one's own time without having to leave home at 6 A.M. to breakfast, or stay out until 8 P.M. for cocktails. Thus, beginning a network can be as simple as setting a routinized lunch date. The ability to control one's time and take an extended lunch for this purpose, in and of itself, may be just the activity the woman executive needs.

Because there are so few women in upper management, an interdisciplinary network has a great deal of utility and appeal. But, the essential question becomes, what will this diverse group of women want? Irrespective of field, these women want career information, peer support, and education. All of them know that despite what male managers and the media may say, women who have risen to the top, in business, academia, or the professions, most likely had no female role models, mentors, or even female supporters.

Peer support is often the first phase of a network group. Peers share like concerns that may range from sexual harrassment, to dressing for success, to learning how to pick up the business luncheon tab. Whatever the degree of support, advice, and information one receives from people who have shared or are currently sharing these issues is validating. One can raise questions that usually may be suppressed out of fear that "I am the only one who does not know."

Career advancement may well be the next phase, once women in the network start to share information about "Who do you know?" and "Where are the next job openings likely to be?" One must constantly be aware that apparently peripheral or irrelevant information and opportunities shared today may be the essentials of a future job move. The goal of education may come from a more formalized speaker's bureau, colloquium series, or newsletter. Networks need not include all these functions and seldom include all from the onset.

For such a structured network, it is important to meet regularly, to keep group membership constant, and to choose a place that is conducive to socialization as well as to business. The dilemma of organizing a group of decisive women may be the reluctance to allow the group process to work. And the group process is likely to take some time because women have not measured each other in the past with respect to career commitments, desire for power, money, and status. That is to say, one must be patient with

the outcomes of the network and not expect hard results (i.e. job information, fundraising strategies, or important connections) immediately. Managerial women, used to operating in isolation and often as targets, may be as
wary of each other as of their business colleagues.

Due to the time necessary for emotional bonding and support to occur,
networks often set up membership criteria and an admission process. If one
or two women create a problem for the others, thereby reducing the
effectiveness of the network, in order to salvage the network, these women
may have to be dropped.

Irrespective of which type of network one develops, some patience is
required to allow group processes to mature. While the longer-term goal
may be to have more focused meetings and discussions on issues of mutual
importance, it may take many months of social chatting first. This open-
ended beginning is a structure that instead of emphasizing one direction
from the start, creates an atmosphere in which growth can take place. One
must remember that these processes engage women with one another in
new ways.

Honesty and confidentiality are also essential ground rules to enable
these supportive networks to function. Each woman must feel secure that
her input will not be repeated and that anything discussed within the
network will remain private and confidential. Although it has been noted
that women tend to be more open than men, in nonaffective areas such as
money, perks, power, and career advancement they are far less open.
However, it is only through this honest sharing, particularly about salaries,
that women will be able to take the assertive steps necessary for salary
negotiations.

BARRIERS TO NETWORKING

It would seem that given these definitions and purposes of networking,
women would rush to initiate or join such groups. The reasons why this does
not happen range from a lack of information about the purposes of such
networks or of those already in existence, to finding the time to participate,
to becoming comfortable with the legitimacy of these groups.

Women's insecurity may be a barrier to networking. They may not
acknowledge their own value and therefore may be uncertain as to what they
have to offer in a reciprocal relationship. It has been noted that, more than
men, women want to relate to others in deep, intense, and lasting ways.
Women in the professional and managerial spheres need to become more
comfortable with the briefer, more detached forms of professional relationships.

Women seem to interpret networking as "using others" and are averse to this notion. Some women are just beginning to become comfortable and to learn that they can "use" (help) each other in mutually productive and supportive ways on the fast track for power. Women need to be comfortable in admitting that they are on the fast track for power, that they are ambitious, and that these goals are acceptable.

External barriers exist as well. Since there are few women in managerial positions, it may be more difficult to identify them and connect with them. One may have to expand the network boundaries to include positions, titles, and responsibilities that are broader in order to have a reasonably diverse group. If networking opportunities fall within the work day (for example, at breakfasts and lunches), the managerial woman must have enough autonomy and flexibility to control her schedule and calendar and to use organizational time to make a commitment to these activities. If such opportunities fall outside the work day (for example, on evenings or weekends), the managerial woman must struggle in a complex hierarchy of priorities and needs to assert the importance of networking and to make time for these activities.

CONCLUSIONS

In conclusion, networking opens doors. It provides role models; provides a channel for information about opportunities that arise; opens up new opportunities for women; and provides an arena in which women can assure one another of their competence to perform (Smith, 1983).

In networking, as in life, you reap what you sow. With awareness of the need for support, information, sharing, and social contact, comes awareness also that women high on the management ladder have difficulty finding female peer networks. Only the most competent female social workers are making it to the top because male employers generally give women less encouragement to train and ask for administrative positions (Sutton, 1982). Until agencies promote women to higher management positions, additional means of maintaining high-level networks could be employed, such as weekend retreats, shared vacations, and informal, area-wide peer group sessions, which would enable women to solve individual problems, ventilate anger, and alleviate stress.

Women need to use the grapevine and make it work for them in the way it works for the "good old boys." If a woman learns of an opening, she should tell other women about it immediately, whether or not the other women express interest. While face-to-face networking is most common, when time or geographic distance is a sufficient barrier, networking can be done through letters, telephone calls, and occasional get-togethers at seminars or conventions. Teleconferencing is also a good tool for the construction and support of network bonds (Smith, 1983).

The enhancing effects on a woman's career and the healthy outlets for organizational ostracism and criticism indicate that all barriers to women's networking should be overcome. Women managers and organizations can work to ensure that women have access to networks and that they use these supports for success. Networking—an important means of gaining power and creating organizational change.

7 Developing a Managerial Style

Sheila has just completed her first presentation on the annual budget. Not only did the board members fail to ask her any substantive questions but, she feels, they dismissed her rather abruptly at the end of the presentation.

What went wrong? she wonders. She carefully prepared and wrote out her entire presentation. She practiced in front of the mirror to make sure that she did not use too many distracting gestures. She even spent an inordinate amount of time in deciding whether to wear her blue pinstripe suit or a gray shirtwaist dress. She carefully chose her jewelry and makeup.

Perhaps some of her uncertainty showed through? In retrospect, she sees that she probably was too serious and overly prepared. Sheila recalls that as she watched the men make their presentations, she noticed the difference between their style and hers. She felt embarrassed for one of them who tried to joke his way through an obviously unprepared presentation.

Who was she supposed to model after? Which style worked? Maybe she needed to bring this topic up at her next women's network group. She would also ask Marsha for advice.

* * *

INTRODUCTION

Recent research suggests that the difference in promotional momentum between men and women might be a result of differential effectiveness related to management styles.

Communication patterns, dress, and leadership style are essential ingredients in effective leadership. To what extent women need to model after the traditional male management styles is greatly debated without consensus.

As indicated earlier, knowing the rules, playing the game, and having the skills and expertise almost guarantees that a competent, ambitious young man will "get someplace" in his career. Not so for women. That same willingness to play, that same competence and skill, will be insufficient to assure advancement and acceptance once she gets there. Male hostility will likely be present, but as an impersonal and subtle force.

Historically women have been excluded from the management hierarchy. So, the fact that they are included in the management labor force does not suggest that they are included in the informal participation of organizational life. However, women's entrance into the management tier has subtly changed the entire organizational game.

For example, studies report differential treatment of managers by their subordinates because of gender (Kravetz & Austin, 1984). These studies mention that men have difficulty in taking direction and constructive criticism from a woman, and that older men have the most difficult time with women as supervisors and directors. An explanation, as noted in Chapter 2, is that these problems may be caused by men's inexperience with female administrators. As such, they are likely to disappear over time. This optimistic view that increased experience with female administrators modifies sexual stereotypical attitudes is given some support by a study in which those managers who were supervised by a woman held more positive views of the managerial skills, abilities, and motivations of women as managers (Ezell, 1982). However, overall, the modification of gender stereotypes is still a future scenario.

While women can develop technical skills related to the initiation and use of management information systems or functional budgeting and they can learn management jargon or computer language, personal management style may not be as easy to learn or alter. More importantly, management style may not be highlighted by the organization or by management training as important.

Working in a position where women are few in numbers puts the woman in the bind: she is expected to be like all other women and at the same time be the exception. Worse yet, her successes are viewed as evidence of being the exception, whereas failures are due to her being like all women (Finkelstein, 1981).

Women who enter the professional landscape with a career in management in mind must consider these issues relative to style and communication. Clearly, they need to purposefully develop a style that will deal constructively with issues regarding communication and management styles.

THE GENERAL ISSUES

What are the issues? Many appear to be related to the socialization process that is so ingrained in men and women. "Being influenced and responding either consciously or unconsciously to the sexuality of the other is the primary way men and women have learned to relate to each other" (Bradford, et al. 1975, p. 42).

Males within an organization can become very confused because organizational roles and consequent appropriate interpersonal interactions cannot now be distinguished on the basis of gender. Now, women are more than secretaries and cleaning ladies, or dates and wives. Game theorists suggest that when any new player enters the game, the dynamics of the entire game change. Consequently, all of the players' moves may become erratic, unpredictable, or even bizarre, and the entire game is altered.

It is important for women managers to remember that the rules have not changed, but the methods of play, the accustomed conduct, and the procedures have deviated from their usual norms. This is particularly disconcerting for the newly arrived woman manager who has just barely learned to negotiate the intricacies of the former behavioral patterns.

The major problem is that women take on the disruption within the organization as their own problems when indeed it is the result of the male player's inability to accept a new and nontraditional player. Consequently, there is no move that a woman can make under these circumstances to calm the situation or to return the chaos back to order, since her behavior did not directly cause the disruption in the first place.

There are other predictable issues for women entering the field of management. To present oneself as a radical feminist who bristles at every sexist joke often alienates co-workers—male and female—and effectively sabotages the image women need to present as a team player. Yet the converse is equally abhorrent, whereby a woman is so insecure that she giggles at every offensive joke in an effort to "get along." By such behavior, she effectively rebuffs advocacy efforts not only for herself, but also for female colleagues in similar positions.

Another issue women managers face involves leadership style. A woman may be considered flirtatious when her only intent is to be friendly, or giddy if she jokes with her male colleagues. Smiling and laughing also can be detrimental to a female in an all-male environment, because in order to be a leader one must be taken seriously. On the other hand, feminists are criticized for taking themselves too seriously and not being able to laugh at themselves.

The literature suggests that the leadership style traditionally associated with the masculine sex-role stereotype continues to be considered effective: decisive, direct, rational, authoritarian, logical, aggressive, and impersonal.

What this suggests is that women's approach to management may be viewed as weak, ineffective, cautious, conciliatory, and subjective.

In our culture there is a general preference for working under the leadership of men, to the extent that many people report an unwillingness to work for a woman. "A preference for men is a preference for power" (Kanter, 1977). People see men as more likely to succeed and gain more power. When a woman acquires power she stops arousing the same level of concern about whether or not she will be wanted as a leader. What appears to be sex differences may really be power differences.

If indeed women are still viewed as powerless, the pragmatic response would be to reject a woman boss. Everyone wants a powerful boss who can advance the interests of the workgroup or organization. While men are comfortable with the young woman fresh out of a master's program as an apprentice or the long-term female employee finally promoted into supervision, they are likely to resent and exclude the woman brought in as an associate executive director or executive director.

The literature suggests that women managers tend to be more controlling of subordinates and in essence to run a tighter ship. However, the explanation for this tendency may be that positions held by women managers typically involve close supervisory hierarchies and concern with detail. Being subjected to bosses who function in a controlling manner, plus the restrictive nature of such bureaucracies decreases the power available to the managers and leads to a controlling style of leadership.

Managing Men

By now it is clear that women who enter the professional landscape with a career in management in mind, must be prepared to deal with many realities. Not only do these realities include male bosses and male colleagues, but they also include male subordinates.

One approach that a woman manager in this situation may try is to soothe the men or to accommodate them. But she is in a "no-win" situation and easily able to exacerbate the organizational upheaval. Some of the corporate literature suggests that women entering these positions recognize that men are threatened by and uncomfortable in these new situations and recommends that women try to understand and be nice to them. It is unfortunate that women often have accepted such advice. In reality, it is more strategically useful for women to capitalize on this discomfort.

Particularly in the very difficult situations of women superiors and male subordinates, old "games" may be played out, initiated by either the woman or the man. Some of these more subtle, but extremely powerful traditional roles may help describe male behaviors toward female executives. They include the common patterns of socialization for both women and men. These traditional roles include:

1. *Macho-male and Seductress roles.* In this dyad, the woman supervisor may affirm her own femininity and give potency to the male, but at the price of being seen as a sex object rather than as a woman with knowledge and managerial skills. In this type of relationship, the woman pours the coffee, the man pulls out the chair and opens the door; the woman takes the minutes, the man runs the meeting.

2. *Helpless Maiden and Chivalrous Knight roles.* This role set allows the woman manager to manipulate her male subordinates by appearing helpless and inept. Unfortunately, it allows the males to view her as weaker and less competent, thereby decreasing the demands and challenges presented to her. In these roles, the woman might pretend an ignorance of budgets or technical equipment, allowing the man to explain, manipulate, or actually perform the job.

3. *Protective Father and the Pet roles.* These roles often develop between an older male subordinate and the younger woman manager. The male takes on the job of protecting the female and the female becomes dependent on him. Consequently, she is typically unable to show her competencies directly, but feels obligated to reflect them through the father figure. Often the woman might credit the man with ideas that she initiated.

4. *Tough Warrior and Nurturant Mother roles.* The male tough warrior is totally self-sufficient and competitive. The nurturing mother manager is valued for the support she can give, rather than for her own abilities and actions. Constructive criticism and logical reasoning are less well-accepted from the nurturing mother. The woman manager in this dyad is valued only when she is complementing the skills and capabilities of the male subordinate.

The solution to the situation is to avoid these traditional roles and to model a new strong and decisive female manager. Obviously, none of these roles strengthens the female manager, or allows her to carve her niche appropriately in the organization.

Communication Styles

Communication usually refers to the exchange of thoughts, through speech, symbols, or writing. It is the process of sending and receiving messages, both verbal and nonverbal. The process is in fact an art. However, like any art form, some individuals are more adept than others. Moreover, as with art, it is subject to different as well as incorrect interpretations. Something as seemingly insignificant as voice intonation or adding a questioning tone to the end of a statement can drastically alter the meaning of a message. These alterations and misinterpretations become even more complex when the sender and receiver of the message are of different genders.

More importantly, the literature on communication indicates that gender-specific nonverbal and verbal behaviors and styles often diffuse the intent of messages and frequently female behaviors in the workplace are misinterpreted. It is critical that a woman manager's communication style not be misinterpreted. This includes the content and presentation style, as well as her nonverbal behaviors.

Research shows that communication styles negatively affect women in individual presentations as well as in group decisional processes. For example, males were found to dominate groups and to challenge others in group situations more quickly than were females (Baird & Bradley, 1979). Since group situations often have a function to perform or task to complete, task-related communication patterns are important to examine. Men are purported to be more task-oriented in groups, while women are viewed to be more socioemotive (Babinic, 1983; Baird & Bradley, 1979; Bales & Slater, 1955). While socioemotive qualities such as openness and emotionality are positive and beneficial in many situations, they may have a negative effect on group interaction by the focus on providing support for others instead of making decisions. These qualities also may have negative repercussions for the woman by their reducing others' perception of her ability to influence the group's decision-making process (Babinec, 1983).

Men were found to be more competitive and to play to win; women, on the other hand, play to keep from losing. Men in group situations also tend to initiate more verbal acts than women (Baird, 1976). Generally, the more verbally active an individual group member is, the more influential that person can be. Men were found to be able to influence both sexes; women could influence neither. The more active and influential an individual is in a group, the more likely he or she will be perceived as a leader.

Verbal Communication

Research indicates that women's speech is less dominant than men's (Henley, 1977), meaning that women tend to ask questions as opposed to making directive statements. They use weaker language, often have softer voices, and are less assertive in the presentation of information and opinions. While many of these "feminine" speech characteristics may be a consequence of early socialization, women are viewed negatively or as less effective managers when adhering to these patterns. However, when a woman uses "masculine" language patterns or styles, she may be viewed as "pushy, aggressive or unfeminine" (Jenkins, 1980, p. 155). Thus if a woman speaks in a loud and very direct manner, she may be considered a "bitch"; if she speaks in a soft and questioning manner, she may be viewed as incapable of making administrative decisions.

Men more often than women engage in back channeling behaviors (that is, they use phrases such as "you're right", "okay") and men take more turns speaking in a management group attended by both sexes (Haynes & Baute, 1986). While the reasons for the differences in these behaviors are unclear, men are more used to team playing and supportive behaviors than women, who may feel that they would appear to be weaker if they supported the positions of others.

In support of the socioemotive nature of women's communication, studies have long purported that women appear to be more self-disclosing than men (Baird & Bradly, 1979; Kuhn, 1982). While this may be advantageous sometimes when compared with the "silent" male norm, it may take on a pejorative connotation for administration since self-disclosure has been associated with behaviors of lower-status individuals, such as the poor and women. Although status differences are not the focus of this chapter, it is worth noting that many of the gender differences in communication do have a dimension that involves status. Whether status is a primary or secondary variable is difficult to assess.

Communication that is open and honest allows the individual to admit doubt or error, a strength in management. It also allows the manager to be comfortable with giving compliments and with listening, not always directing.

Nonverbal Communication

Whenever there is a discrepancy between verbal and nonverbal communication, the nonverbal component is given much credence by both men and women. This has tremendous implications for women in the workplace. Women maintain eye contact for longer periods, and women value more highly the information they receive through eye contact (Cahill, 1981; Baird, 1976). However, different interpretations are given to this behavior according to gender. Prolonged eye contact or gazing is often misinterpreted by men as "courting cues" or flirting. Men, therefore, may respond with some other intimate behavior. Consequently, managerial women may maintain eye contact to make a point and thus be unfairly labeled as a "tease."

Certainly if women's verbal and nonverbal behaviors are more congruous than men's and if they were received as such, their style would engender more trust by their superiors as well as subordinates. In contrast, men's styles may leave others more confused by the mixed messages they communicate.

Differences between males and females in the number of body movements also have been observed and studied. Postural shifts and self-adaptors (e.g., adjusting clothing, "fixing" hair, or stroking beard) occur more frequently in males (Frances, 1979). In other words, men move more, touch themselves more, and adjust their clothing more than women. This may seem contradictory to the commonly held notion that women fidget with jewelry, smooth their hair, and file their fingernails. The literature and research suggest, however, that these movements by men may be deliberate attempts to draw attention to themselves. An alternate explanation may be that women have been socialized to sit still and not draw attention to themselves, whereas men are more comfortable with moving. Neither gender may view their behaviors as planned or effective.

Studies of proxemics (Cahill, 1981; Goffman, 1966; Summer, 1969) present evidence that relative to men's space, women's space is more closely invaded by both men and women. If, as the research indicates, women are more "open," then it follows that being approached more closely or demanding less space is further evidence of that openness. Holding one's own space is essential for an administrator; conversely, giving up one's space may be construed as a sign of deference. It is not unusual to see male managerial colleagues approach each other at a meeting and shake hands. It is also not unusual to see a male managerial colleague approach a female managerial colleague and give her a hug.

Differences also exist in the degree or amount of touching exhibited and initiated by men and women. Males initiate touching toward females much more than toward other males. Further, men are more likely to attach a sexual meaning to being touched by women, than are women who are touched by men (Henley, 1977). This finding may be further evidence of women's tendency to be more open.

Research indicates that girls are touched and held more than boys, which may result in women being more comfortable with physical contact and may explain the apparent discomfort that men experience concerning touching (Goldberg & Lewis, 1969). These socialization patterns could contribute to men's attributing sexual connotations to physical touching or close proximity. Furthermore, these findings may suggest that female managers who touch colleagues and employees to emphasize a point risk their action being misconstrued as a sexual overture. Therefore, women managers may need to make significant changes in such behavioral patterns.

While any type of communication transaction is constrained without some degree of smiling or laughing, too much smiling detracts from the situation. Perpetual smiling or laughing may cause confusion and detract from the serious intent of the message. Women are especially vulnerable to this since the managerial domain is predominantly populated by males—to be taken seriously is imperative.

Women, however, have been found to laugh and smile much more during conversations than men (Goffman, 1966). As previously noted, to the extent that women are more socioemotive and open than men, laughing or smiling may be related characteristics. Women often smile during conversations due to nervousness. Since women are relatively new to management and are often the lone female in a managerial group, these situations may be especially conducive to uneasiness or uncertainty. Smiling or laughing, however, may be considered by men as part of the stereotypical "female giddiness," and therefore viewed as detrimental to effective management. However, the other side is a woman who is too serious; she will be ridiculed for being too "uptight."

Written Communication

Studies of the differences in male and female writing styles are inconclusive, although many indicate that women use more formal terms in writing. For example, women tend to use cannot as opposed to can't or would not as opposed to wouldn't. Additionally, women tend to be less assertive in written communication. More than male writers they tend to use more hedging (e.g., I feel, I think, or I believe) (Forisha & Goldman, 1981). This characteristic seems to indicate that women are not as confident in their presentation of information. Another explanation may be that women's inclination to be open and to accept others' opinions might be an impediment to their presentation of information as fact. These characteristics could be especially detrimental in intraoffice memorandum where the phraseology may appear to persuade or cajole, rather than to direct.

Personality Characteristics

While pejorative comments are often made about the nurturing and empathetic qualities of women, these qualities also can be seen as important and useful for management. On the one hand, it is dysfunctional for employees to view the female executive as a "mommy," because they will expect her door to always be open, that she will not take a task-oriented perspective, and that she will not be decisive. On the other hand, when these nurturing qualities are appropriately brought to administration, they may well "humanize" the workplace and enhance employee morale.

These characteristics are conducive to an investment in workers, thereby supporting employee development and supportive services. Women can and do better appreciate the dual roles of employees relative to family and career. These characteristics will likely increase the female executive's commitment to staff participation in decision making, to cooperation and collaboration among workers as opposed to hierarchical and competitive structures, and to valuing process as well as outcome.

Women tend to have more concern with the quality of the work environment, in improving the physical work conditions, and being cognizant of and sensitive to inequities at the workplace (Kravetz & Austin, 1984). In the long run, these characteristics are not contradictory to effective leadership and organizational performance.

Dress

Yet another area of difficulty in managerial style for women is dress. Since there is no "uniform" for the human service agency, it may be even more difficult for women in this field than in either business or industry where dress codes, at least for men, may be more standardized. Women managers do not need to look like men, devoid of any femininity or personal style. However, they do need to examine their workplace and be certain that they are not dressing like the support personnel (Molloy, 1977).

Under no circumstances in the world of work should women dress like the seductress, cheerleader, or housewife. Excess in anything—makeup, jewelry, hairstyle, fads in clothing—should be avoided. Calling attention to one's body instead of one's skills and abilities projects an adverse message in the workplace.

What the successful woman manager in human services needs to personify is a combination of presence and authority with approachability. A too-tailored and severe look may not only appear imitative of men, but may also suggest that she is unapproachable. A tailored suit with a blouse with a frill at the neck or a soft dress with a jacket are combinations that meet the standard. While grays and dark blues are the common and accepted colors of the workplace, many others can be used effectively. A tailored pink wool suit may be the most appropriate outfit with which to project the qualities of the successful woman manager.

Often human service managers must influence members of the business community. The power of that group and its norms for dressing should be taken into account to assure respect. In other words, thinking ahead about one's day and activities should suggest the appropriate type of dress. First impressions may well be lasting ones.

CONCLUSIONS

It is evident that differences exist between male and female managerial styles. However, the conclusion most frequently reached that women need to take on the male model is simply an outdated and biased prescription. Many benefits are derived from the female styles of management.

To succeed in the world of management, women must realize that

1. Male hostility is impersonal and subtle.
2. Women are viewed as unwanted intruders in a previously safe male enclave.
3. Women need to learn the game rules.
4. Women can take control by capitalizing on male discomfort (Harragan, 1984).

Education and socialization are needed for individuals in the workplace to become accustomed to and comfortable with varying styles. Moreover, it is necessary for them to measure effective outcomes through mechanisms other than the behaviors observed. While such steps would enable women to be cognizant of the differences in style, they should not automatically adapt to these differences. Employees ought to be able to recognize as effective an array of managerial styles. They also should recognize the potential strength in using a variety of styles within the same organization, relative to different situations and groups in the organization.

Both men and women should recognize these differences, however, and attempt to adjust in order to more effectively work together. Studies demonstrate that once women are in the workplace individual differences are more apparent. However, with time and an increase of women in managerial positions these differences not only seem to be more accepted, but also seem to be more appreciated. The danger remains that women will be given midmanagement positions and forced to remain in such positions. Therefore, it is imperative that women and men prevent communication styles from becoming barriers to organizational advancement.

Developing, modifying, and assessing one's own management style and retaining a sense of perspective is essential to anyone's success. It is particularly so for the "token" and isolated female manager. The provisions for success lie in better understanding the messages sent out, and in modifying those according to tasks or activities.

8 High Tech and High Finance

Sheila looks at the job description of a managerial position two levels above her position, which has become vacant unexpectedly. She knows that given her thorough understanding of her present job and the success of the programs she administers, she would probably be a strong candidate for the position.

She also is eager to experience several aspects of the job: engaging in more interagency collaboration and working more with the media. She would also be in charge of a multimillion dollar budget, of making budget projections for long timeframes, and of fundraising and negotiating for grants and contracts. The latter responsibilities frighten her.

She calms herself by recalling how well she handles her current budget of a half-million dollars. But it's a simple one, she argues. She only has to monitor salaries, benefits, and a small amount for operating expenses. She cannot transfer funds across lines, is not required to project this budget more than one year in advance, and is not responsible for generating the dollars.

She closes her eyes to view herself in this position. Interestingly, her first setback is her inability to see herself in the large, carpeted office. That aside, she sees herself sitting at the computer next to the desk with a spread sheet in front of her. A programmer is showing her the intricacies of this new, faster, more advanced database program. He talks rapidly as he presses a few function keys that make the numbers on the budget sheet jump.

He is explaining how simple it is to experiment with a few "what if" scenarios before making a budget presentation. For example, what if the legislature were to mandate an 8 percent across-the-board salary increase for all staff at the same time that the fees for service were increased by $5.00 per hour. Or, what if the United Way allocation were to increase by 20 percent, salaries by 3 percent, and the health benefit allowance by 28 percent?

The programmer leaves the office with the parting words, "It'll make your life so much more simple." In a panic, Sheila watches him leave.

Out of her daydream and back to reality, she wonders if David, the incumbent in the position, ever felt intimidated by the high technology or the high finance. Did he ask questions? Did he stumble through? How would she ever know?

* * *

INTRODUCTION

Historically and currently women have been stereotyped as having no abilities, interest, or education in either technology or finance. Indeed, in the human services, neither are taught in the curriculum of graduate or undergraduate programs, and it has taken human service agencies some time to "catch up" with the technology and budgetary standards of the private profit-making sector. Thus, the dilemma for women in human services is twofold: (1) high tech and high finance are usually not part of their educational and socialization experience during their preparation for a human service career and (2) women are not expected to know anything about these traditionally male areas.

The human services continue to stress process and social interaction skills much more than they emphasize the business aspects of organizational structuring and management. In contrast, the interest in human relations management within the last decade in the business sector places emphasis on humanizing the workplace, on participatory decision making, and on employee-centered issues. As already noted, there are a multitude of explanations for the high proportion of women who enter social work and the relatively low percentage of these women who reach senior-level management ranks. Another possible explanation is that women choose social work for the compatibility of its values and processes with their own values and socialization. Management in human services, therefore, may appear to reverse the importance of these values and skills and, consequently, may be of lesser interest to women.

FINANCE

Salaries

Probably the initial difficulty regarding finance rests with the issue of women making their own money. Historically, most women have been socialized to expect to be taken care of—through trust funds, wealthy fathers, or highly paid spouses. "Real ladies" could and still can afford to be crusaders, helpers of the poor, guardians of the culture, and patrons of the arts—much as were the original "Lady Bountifuls." Women without money still devote themselves to social and artistic causes, but at great sacrifices, greater even than they themselves admit. Were it not for these women, boards of social agencies would be greatly diminished in size, time for volunteer work, and talent.

Well-educated women from middle- and upper-income families still think of themselves as comfortably well-off, even when their incomes barely exceed the poverty level. The problem is that women and men still look at serious money making (not pocket money) by women as an activity of the greedy or the unfeminine. For example, one of the unfortunate arguments raised against comparable worth is that a woman may be married to a man who earns a salary and thus she does not "need" as much. Add to this the altruistic message of the social work profession, and it becomes easier to recognize that women may feel guilty about earning competitive wages.

Certainly many women face salary issues related to starting out too low and then falling behind quickly. Several years later, the inequities are too great for a small adjustment to make a difference. In negotiations regarding salaries, women may concede that they have insufficient experience, do not possess the skills required for the next level, or have a "healthy family income."

Additionally, questions such as "What were you paid on your last job?" or "What do you think you're worth?" can pose difficulties for women. Some women may discount their ability to take on new roles and tasks, or may feel like imposters in the management hierarchy, or may be underpaid. These women cannot, without new skills and self-confidence, artfully and successfully negotiate the larger salaries of upper management.

No woman aspiring to management can be uncomfortable with salary negotiations and merit increments. Initial salary negotiations as well as ongoing review for merit allocations are essential financial areas of management. Operationalizing criteria and translating those into salary dollars are ongoing tasks for any manager.

As women move up the management ladder, expense accounts are not only perks, but necessary to conduct business—more business lunches and out-of-town travel may become necessary. Women may be prone to consider these as luxuries or as unnecessary. Given that some women may have used out-of-pocket monies for such activities, they may feel it is unethical to charge the organization.

Therefore, it is important for women to find answers to the questions that arise about many of the gray areas of expense accounts. Should the agency pay for my professional dues? Can I charge a business lunch if it is with a friend? If the friend is a professionally useful individual the lunch does indeed concern business. But, would a business lunch be legitimate if you considered the future potential usefulness of an acquaintance?

If the agency does not have a set per diem, women may struggle about what is fair and reasonable. In business, the rule of thumb is the high end of the dinners at the restaurant at your hotel or a comparable hotel is acceptable. Taxis and tips are usual, legitimate expenses. Whether alcoholic beverages, dry cleaning charges, or tips to porters are considered legitimate depends on the individual agency's policy. Entertaining at home, if it appears to be part of the job, involves expense account items. Invitations to social events due to one's position and which will benefit the agency are part of the politics of management positions. The costs of bringing a spouse to these events should be discussed and will most likely be included.

Budgets

Women's traditional fear of numbers has kept many of them out of better paying jobs that require the management of large budgets. The research demonstrating that in tests of mathematical skills females generally score lower than males does not suggest that the differential is biologically predetermined, but that it is the result of sex-role conditioning. Young women are often discouraged from pursuing mathematics, are not expected to do well in this area, and are afraid that with success in mathematics they will be perceived as unfeminine.

Most women have experience, professionally and personally, with handling budget decisions, balancing accounts, and keeping ledgers current. While all of the accounting terms may not be familiar, the concepts of line item and lump-sum budgets are known and understood by program managers as well as by household managers. An MBA degree is not needed to recognize that expenses and revenues ought to balance and that cautious budget projections include a conservative estimate on the revenue side and a liberal estimate on the expense side.

Women have to internalize the idea that budgets operationalize the goals of organizations. And, as such, budgets should reflect the priorities set with respect to program outcomes and employee satisfaction and performance. Viewed from this perspective, multimillion dollar budgets become no more frightening than personal budgets. Women, particularly those in human services, may see budgets as being too precise and as inadequately reflecting the true value of service or the true outcome of that service. However, when at least some of the evaluation of service delivery is represented to federal and state legislators and to private donors as cost for unit of service delivered or for clients helped, it is essential that the budget is accurately interpreted.

Another difficulty women face concerns the belief that one needs expertise in accounting to understand budgets and to designate revenues and expenditures into the appropriate line item or fund balance. Large or small, cash or accrual accounting, basic issues of cash flow, deficits, or profits remain the same. Knowing whether items are recurring costs, should be allocated to administrative overhead or operating expenses does not require special expertise.

The ability to say no to unrealistic requests, to provide sufficient financial incentives, and to reward subordinates differentially are skills not usually highlighted in graduate education.

TECHNOLOGY

Similarly, women continue to believe and consequently perpetuate the idea that technology is too difficult for them to master or that it is too unfeminine. Yet, many of the traditionally female roles and occupations continue to use technology as a central component.

Nurses, for example, must understand and utilize an array of machines, which are increasingly complex and sophisticated, ranging from X-ray and blood pressure machines to monitors on cardiac patients to MRI (magnetic response imagery) machines. On a daily basis, school teachers use audio-visual equipment, computerized examinations, and computer-instructed learning.

Cosmeticians and beauticians use increasingly complex technology in their trade. Bank tellers and salesclerks rely on computers in all transactions. Secretaries (mostly women) have mastered the manual typewriters of yesteryear and the present-day word processors and computers, not to mention dictaphones, intercoms, and highly intricate telephone systems.

Women in the home master conventional and microwave ovens, dishwashers, sewing machines, food processors, VCRs (videocassette recorders), telephone-answering machines, and home-beauty equipment without a second thought.

The utilization of technology in these areas has long been sanctioned and encouraged by men, whereas in business (and now in human service management), the use of technology is viewed as unfeminine. Perhaps the contradiction between women's abilities and their attitudes concerning technology stems from their exclusion from the more desirable, higher paying positions.

Administrators in human service agencies certainly do not deal with anything more complex than the equipment already mentioned. Computer technology is now used by many human service agencies to more efficiently store and analyze management information, client information, and human service resource information. Many human service agencies rely on sophisticated telephone equipment, audiovisual equipment, and security systems. However, nowhere is the human service manager expected to operate these systems without training or without support.

BREAKING THE MYTH

In order to break these myths, women must not only realize that they already have mastered many of the skills related to high finance and high technology, but women also must realize that men do not necessarily feel comfortable and skilled in these areas either. The major difference is that men do not admit their discomfort or lack of knowledge and skills. Men often have "girls" to master some of these skills for them—for example, their secretaries and administrative assistants. Moreover, when men make mistakes in these areas, they can admit them, make light of them, and move on.

Women also need to recognize that it is difficult for everyone to keep up with technology since the state of the art changes so rapidly, with hardware and software constantly improving. They must learn that the higher up in administration one moves, the more probable it becomes that one will have staff to rely on to interpret information, to perform the complicated accounting, and to explain the new software. This reliance on staff for the specialized knowledge and skills related to high finance or budgets is no different than the reliance on expert personnel for substantive or programmatic knowledge.

CONCLUSION

Above all in job negotiations, women need to be clear about what the job needs in the way of talent and expertise and what they are worth to the organization. They cannot be influenced by what they might be paid at the time, or by family income, or by a potential employer's attempts to bargain downward.

Women need to be equally skillful in recognizing the hidden expenses contained in management positions, such as entertaining, travel, and being at the "right" events. To the extent that these are necessary and expected parts of the position, they ought to be covered. Negotiating liberal expense accounts, not only in the dollars available, but in the discretionary expenditure of them, is important to successfully complete the job.

Women must learn about financing, accounting, and budgeting as preparation for senior-management positions and for their own self-confidence. One can buy simple books or take seminars to acquire at least a working knowledge of these matters. In order to gain experience as well as knowledge, women should request tasks related to these areas early in their career in preparation for advancement.

Women need to understand that managers do not need to be financiers and accountants, but that they do need to understand enough to direct subordinates in tasks and to analyze reports. Additionally, all finance systems have checks and balances; therefore, if one makes a mistake, another department or individual is likely to find it and correct it.

Women must realize that budgets and finance are and will continue to be an important aspect of management. If women perceived budgets as the operationalization of the organization's goals and not as a mystery, of budgetary control as power, and of accounting as the job for accountants, many problems would disappear.

Just as in the area of budgets, women need to prepare themselves with information and experience in the area of technology. Women cannot afford to fear requesting consultation, training, or review of performance in this area. The woman manager need not know how to fix a computer or a telephone, but she must know the capabilities of the equipment.

Technology will continue to advance so rapidly that very few people can stay knowledgeable. Consequently, one needs to be well-informed concerning the equipment and the needs of the organization. One need choose the most advanced equipment only when necessary.

Women need to understand that technology will increase in use and sophistication as the importance of cost-effectiveness and efficiencies increase in the social service arena. The myths that machines are unfeminine and that women managers only intuit and do not need data are erroneous and must be dispelled.

Issues related to high finance and advanced technology also will continue to be of concern to human services. Women's preparation for advancement to senior-level management positions, therefore, must take this into account and build in knowledge as well as experience.

It should be clear that these issues are relevant not only to women managers, but to men as well. Myths regarding women's abilities in finance and technology serve to consign women to lower-management positions and should be seen as such.

9 Putting It All Together

Jan looks at her watch and then at the calendar. It's only 2 P.M., but she is exhausted. Next week will be her fortieth birthday and she is dreading it. She cannot imagine why she is in such a negative mindset lately. Usually she is upbeat and optimistic. But the pile of papers on her desk—budget revisions, personnel evaluations, and a grant proposal—is mounting. Working late is impossible because she has tickets for the symphony tonight.

If Jan were to take an objective look at her daily life—not just her day—perhaps she would understand the stress. This morning, up at 5:45 A.M. as usual, she cooked breakfast for the family, tested her daughter for the weekly spelling test, visited the post office to mail the 100 invitations to her upcoming fortieth birthday party, and wrote instructions for the part-time housekeeper. For lunch, she ate yogurt at her desk while reading the report for this afternoon's management meeting.

Last night, she telephoned three babysitters when the regular sitter canceled at the last minute. And, yesterday, her dearest friend entered a hospital in a city 150 miles away for relatively minor surgery. Yet, Jan is engulfed in guilt, for not being a good friend and driving up to see her.

Jan's week is usually as hectic. Perhaps this frantic pace explains her lack of excitement at spending the evening with her husband at the symphony.

Jan is convinced that successful and talented women should have no difficulty with a major life passage—turning 40 years of age. Yet she is facing this celebratory event with some concern, and, worse yet, is worried that an "o.k." woman should face this life passage with only excitement.

What is wrong? She has an excellent management job and is

extremely skilled at what she does. She always keeps herself well-groomed and has a loving husband and children who seem to be models of good behavior.

* * *

INTRODUCTION

There is certainly nothing wrong with wanting it all. The difficulty is in attaining it all—on a basis equal with men and without supports. In the late 1970s the term "superwoman" was used to describe women like Marsha. Commercials portrayed these women as follows:

> Superwoman prepares a well-balanced, nutritional breakfast, which her children eat. She goes off to work where she makes at least $30,000 a year as an executive of a law firm. She comes home and reads to the children and then serves dinner, by candlelight, to her husband (Shaevitz, 1984, p. 2).

The major problem with superwomen is their failure to recognize that the making of one choice limits other choices. Combining professional and personal roles demands compromise and balance; and success in one area may entail some loss in others. Women must learn to acknowledge their limits, to accept responsibility for their decisions, and to forgive themselves for being only human after all.

It is understandable that superwomen become trapped by "I-can-do-it-all" complexes. Female executives, as few as there are, usually complain that they work more hours per week than their male counterparts and feel that they make personal or family sacrifices for the sake of their careers. Most successful male executives indicate that personal and family sacrifices generally accompany a business career.

DEFINITION

The superwoman syndrome includes a range of physical, psychological, and interpersonal stress symptoms experienced by a woman as she attempts to perform "perfectly" multiple and conflicting roles as worker, wife, mother, homemaker, friend. The physical symptoms of stress related to the superwoman syndrome include headaches, tension in neck, shoulder, or back, and menstrual irregularities; psychological symptoms include feeling overextended or overwhelmed, feeling pressure, anxious, and difficulty in sleeping; and interpersonal symptoms include irritability with co-workers, children, or partner and working harder with less effectiveness.

The first challenge to women to be superwomen began in 1963, with Betty Friedan's *The Feminine Mystique*. This book included two major thrusts: (1) for women to gain greater control over their lives, including their bodies and (2) for women to gain greater access to all aspects of the working world. Many women since that time have entered the labor force, not necessarily to gain access to greater control and power, but due to economic necessity.

Women now are expected to be the "perfect" employee or boss, but society has not changed its expectations for women also to be the "perfect" wife, mother, and friend. Furthermore, both research and experience reveal that for a woman to succeed in the business and professional world, she must be more competent, more committed, more efficient, and more effective than any man at her current job level or at a higher job level.

Increasingly, women try to "have it all" and do it all simultaneously. Women want careers, spouses, families, friends, and time for themselves and their hobbies and sports. What women fail to realize is that men do not "have it all." Men too often give up spending time with families for the fast track in their careers; invest little time in friends; and spend time in sports or hobbies to the detriment of significant relationships. Particularly given the rise in the number of female-headed households, women need to take heed of the warning signals of the superwoman.

There are several factors—internal and external—that identify super-women or potential superwomen. External factors include how many multiple roles a woman holds simultaneously: professional, wife, mother, daughter, friend, mentor. Internal factors include how much guilt she feels, how difficult it is to say "no," the level of stress or depression, and the degree of "niceness orientation."

To determine if you are in danger of experiencing this syndrome, begin by asking yourself if you want to:

> feel good about yourself?
> have more time for yourself, for people who are important to you, for relaxation and fun?
> have more time for your partner; to have a warm and caring relationship?
> have happy, independent, competent children who have high self-esteem?
> have work that you enjoy?
> make money?
> be physically healthy?
> have close, nurturing friends?
> have a home that is a haven rather than a demand list? (Shaevitz, 1984, p. 16).

If the answers to many of these questions are yes and the reality is no, then you must work on juggling and balancing the multiple expectations so that a comfortable fit is found. You also must let go of the need to be "perfect" in every area. If you are already an overachiever on the job and answer yes to most of the questions, it is essential to prioritize and balance these needs and desires. Only in that way can you create a healthy balance rather than a stressful, no-win struggle.

ESSENTIAL COMPONENTS TO BALANCE

Job

In the earlier chapter on career development, many important questions are raised relative to choosing a career and an organization that is compatible with one's priorities, personality, lifestyle, and skills (Collins, 1984; York, Henley, & Gamble, 1985). Clearly, these major choices—when addressed early, reevaluated often, and acted on—will permit one to more easily balance competing demands.

However, no career or job is without complexities. For instance, intensive work may be required for a time-limited period, requiring a different, but temporary reassessment of priorities. If unexpected, one must then consider saying no to the increased demands, given the problems that may occur in other areas. One also must evaluate the benefits of saying yes, such as promotions, skills learned, and visibility. Whenever possible, take at least one day to consider no or yes responses and talk with a friend or with a mentor.

Partners

Women executives most frequently note that their jobs deprive them of important personal time. Not surprisingly, much of the literature suggests that the success of many women's balancing of career and family rests with her choice of a spouse. Most women executives choose husbands with social and economic backgrounds similar to their own; that is, husbands in professional and managerial jobs.

Men associated with superwomen complain most about the complexities of their lives and express some sense of disappointment at not being cared for enough. Many feel that their superwoman partners are not available to them except when "everything else gets done."

While intimate relationships take hard work, they also can be extremely wonderful, loving, and rewarding. It is important to examine a series of male-female relationship models in order to determine whether women idealize relationships that cannot coexist with a professional career.

Too many women continue to fantasize about the "traditional" relationship, which may model their parents' relationship. In this relationship, the male is the breadwinner, senior decisionmaker, powerful, and unemotional. The female is the full-time homemaker, child caregiver, and nurturer. She bakes cookies for the PTA; car pools the children to school, tennis, piano and dance lessons, and friends' homes; and keeps house. She is depicted as personifying the "perfect" female role. Not only is this model clearly impossible for the woman employed full-time outside the home, it is seldom "perfectly" fulfilled by the full-time homemaker. The homemaker often spends more time cleaning the toilets than baking cookies, or overscheduling bridge and tennis games as to be unavailable for car pools.

Another model constantly idealized in the media is the romantic relationship, in which the everyday trivialities of dishes, garbage, and food shopping are absent as well as the everyday existence of jobs, children, and friends. Women fantasize about the intensity of these relationships, often forgetting that men may view this behavior as only courting behavior. Women lucky enough to find companions who continue to require and give intimacy may be surprised at the amount of time and energy such intimacy costs. Preparing and serving romantic dinners by candlelight almost every night after a strenuous ten-hour workday and a commute home in rush-hour traffic takes its toll.

Another common expectation involves "best buddy," in which the partner is not only expected to be a best friend, but the only friend. This puts an incredible strain on the relationship and sets up the pair for disappointment. Working women and their partners need to realize that a balance in multiple colleagues and friends reduces, rather than increases, the strain on the relationship.

An increasingly appealing model to working women is the equal partnership model, in which both partners share equally in all responsibilities and resources. The catch: partners think that equality can exist without a great deal of planning, compromise, and miscommunication. Additionally, if the partners' resources are unequal, they may feel that the benefits also should be distributed unequally.

Many women in the current labor force are torn. They saw in their parents the traditional relationship, but want for themselves something closer to the equal partnership model. Unfortunately, they do not see other models in between these two extremes.

Children

Since the 1960s and the reality of planned pregnancy, career women are faced with one of the most critical, emotional, and individual decisions of their lives. Arguments abound for (1) delaying childbearing until career development is well underway; (2) delaying careers until children are in school all day; (3) simultaneously going forward with both; and (4) choosing between childbearing and full-time careers. Many women must face reality in that the luxury of sequencing is impossible. That is, marrying later may make unrealistic the further delay of childbearing.

Career women must acknowledge that quality mothering need not be a full-time job and that many aspects of the traditional mothering role can be allocated to extended family, friends, partners, and paid child caregivers. Also, as all parents come to realize, children's expectations can and usually will expand to the limits of the parent's willingness to meet them.

Children need love, affection, and some time with a parent or parents. As children become older, they need less attention to their physical needs and more attention to their emotional development. Parents can usually successfully attend to such needs in the evenings and on weekends. Therefore, parents who feel fulfilled in their life choices and not guilty about them, can more freely and fully give to their children.

Friends

Friendships require attention and time, as do all relationships. Working women continue to report, however, that frequently friendship receives a low priority in their lives. Working full time, which in management may include evening and weekend meetings, leaves little free time. Women feel guilty if they do not allocate that time to partners, children, and managing the house. It is not uncommon for women friends, living in the same town, not to see each other for months and to try frantically to catch up by telephone. Even friends who may be important from a networking perspective are often a very low priority.

Women must remember that friends provide supportive personal networks, the opportunity to ventilate, and the chance to share joys and sorrows. Friendships are necessary; they allow women to maintain that uneasy balance between professional demands and personal time. Without placing friendships as a higher priority, women's ability to balance competing demands may be too difficult.

Community

Particularly in the field of human services, volunteer work in the community not only emanates from a woman's need to improve her community, but also from expectations within the field and perhaps her organization. The human service manager takes on leadership functions in the community by serving on boards of directors of not-for-profit agencies, accepting appointments to blue-ribbon committees, working on task forces, and so on. These activities are essential prerequisites to the manager's moving into the position of executive director. Therefore, these obligations, which are not directly addressed in the job description, further reduce a woman's expendable time and are included in the juggling act.

Self

Often, the personal needs of the woman herself are at the bottom of the list of priorities. How many working women feel guilt if they leave the office early to get a haircut, or to see the dentist? Managerial men frequently play golf or tennis on company time and acknowledge that such time is useful for networking. Men in management also express little concern for making doctor's and barber's visits on company time, because they recognize that evenings and often weekends are spent in work-related activities.

Rather than feeling guilt, women—superwomen in particular—must learn to say no to certain obligations. They must take time to relax, sit in a hot bath, read a novel for an evening, or spend an entire Sunday in bed reading magazines. Rather than focusing on the needs of others, women must learn to prioritize their own needs.

DECIDING WHAT'S IMPORTANT

The only way to avoid the chaos and fatigue of the superwoman syndrome is to determine what is important in your life and to prioritize your time accordingly.

Guilt is commonly described as being remorseful for a wrongdoing. As noted, superwomen feel guilty if they do not take care of everybody else's needs *and* they feel guilty if they take care of their own needs.

Guilt is an unproductive emotion; guilty feelings and guilt-ridden behaviors waste energies that would be better spent taking care of oneself and enjoying life. It is counterproductive to feel guilty about working late one night, when doing so makes one feel productive and consequently, more able to enjoy one's family. The point is to make the choices and live with them—without guilt.

Another important factor in feeling out of control is a lack of assertiveness. Assertiveness is defined as a "compelling recognition of one's needs." Often, assertiveness is confused with aggression. Women must learn to assert themselves by saying no and by asking for help. However, because of their orientation to the needs of others, assertive behavior is difficult. Moreover, superwomen want to be liked, need to constantly affirm their capabilities, and come close to paralysis in asking for help. Women's inability to assert themselves adds up to the solo woman doing it all, perfectly, for everyone.

In making these choices to reprioritize for the longer timeframe, and in reexamining them in the shorter timeframe, women must recognize and accept that making choices has consequences. To the extent that women realize that "having it all" perfectly and at the same time is not possible, then making the choices must involve benefits and costs. While women have fought discrimination on the job for decades and argued for comparable worth, some women (as well as some men) interpret this push for equity to mean that women should be able to have it all without any price. Men do not have it all: they have been forced by society to make choices and to feel less guilty about their decisions.

Women who choose to take time out of the labor force and their careers to spend in full-time parenting should not expect to enter the labor force at the same place as other women their same age who continued their careers. Delayed or interrupted entry in the labor force has consequences—as does uninterrupted employment—on the amount of time available for children.

THE BALANCING ACT

The balancing act quite clearly requires many of the same skills of management, although women fail to see their applicability and transferability. For example, the reoccurring theme of "not enough time" can be remedied by applying the same time-management skills of the workplace.

Superwomen tend to believe that with "enough" time they could "do it all." However, the issue may involve their ability to reallocate time and to delegate responsibilities to gain "quality" time. Many of the tasks women perform can be done by others—children, partner, paid housekeeper—or can go undone. Hard as it is to "let go," some tasks can wait. For instance, vacuuming the entire house once a week may keep it tidy, but is not essential if personal time is being shortchanged.

Time management is an essential talent in the attempt to balance competing demands. Women, therefore, need to concentrate on this technique to reduce stress. For example, women continue to believe that they must work harder than men to be as successful. Although hard work is necessary for success, despite such commitment failure does occur. Overall, success involves knowing what is necessary to get ahead and recognizing what is not essential.

Similarly, good managers delegate tasks to appropriate subordinates with operational definitions, timelines, and specified outcomes. This management skill is essential for the woman manager attempting to balance the multitude of competing tasks in her life. The woman manager's inability to delegate tasks to subordinates, a partner, or children may not only prevent her from succeeding (by an overload of duties), but also may prevent those subordinates or family members from learning new skills, feeling competent, and exhibiting supportive behaviors.

Women exert unnecessary pressures on themselves by refusing to delegate tasks on the job or at home because they fear that delegation indicates failure or lack of competence. Likewise, women tend to say "yes" to tasks that are unimportant or tangential to their job, goals, or skills. By carefully maintaining time for their priorities, women can increase their productivity and satisfaction.

Many women executives carry an appointment book and meticulously keep all meetings. Many, however, fail to schedule time for themselves, their partners, and recreation. Another important point to remember is that one should not schedule a meeting just because there is vacant time on the calendar, without first asking whether the meeting suits professional or personal goals.

Time for oneself is notoriously last on most women's lists. Yet it is an important component of retaining the ability to move forward, to motivate others, and to be optimistic. Taking one afternoon a month for pampering—whether to get a new hairstyle, or a manicure, facial, or massage—is no more luxurious than attending a half-day seminar on employee motivation or the latest in word processing.

Women also complain about their need for nurturing. While not making demands, women must verbalize their expectations concerning nurturing and express their needs. Perhaps unrealistically, women want nurturing, but without requesting it. Comparable management roles include the clear articulation of tasks, behaviors, and outcomes expected from subordinates. Management literature constantly stresses this technique, yet women tend to disregard its applicability to their personal lives.

Thus, women need to learn how to negotiate successfully for what they want and need, both on and off the job. Negotiation means knowing how to persuade as well as how to say no. It also requires that women accept the reality of someone saying no, and that they then make the decision to pursue it or to let it go.

COPING WITH SUCCESS

Hand-in-hand with the superwoman syndrome is the imposter phenomenon—women who are unable to hear the compliments of others and who cannot accept the objective evidence regarding their success or ability. Paradoxically, these same women desperately want to know that they are competent, well-liked, and respected.

These women are not exhibiting false modesty, but really feel that others have a false impression of them. While it is easy to understand people's fear of failure, it is more difficult to understand people's fear of success. For women, fear of success is further exacerbated by the notion that "I'm not entitled to success" and "I must not outdo dad."

Fear of success leads women to believe that they fool people, because they are not what they appear to be. Not surprisingly, then, these women live in fear that they will be exposed as frauds. Such symptoms of fear may arise at one period in life and not be constant; women can overcome them. These feelings and symptoms can also apply to interpersonal relationships if one feels like a fraud. That is, "perfect" friends or wives give support when it is needed and say yes to all requests. If they are not "perfect," they may feel like imposters (Clance, 1985; Imes & Clance, 1984).

By understanding these feelings, acknowledging them, and realizing that they are not objective truth, one can stop such behaviors. One is more likely to reduce symptoms by (1) the knowledge that self-satisfaction is important and (2) identifying whom and in what situations it is necessary to please.

Another difficulty in this balancing act for successful women managers is how to deal with success. Women in intimate relationships or who want such relationships need to consider with their partner the following questions:

What happens when the man reaches a low point just at the moment when his partner achieves success?

What happens when the woman's success requires that the man move with her to another community?

What happens when a woman's behavior changes markedly because of her success?

What happens when her success is sudden and unanticipated?

Conflicts are likely to arise when role reversals occur. For instance, a relationship in which the woman earns more money and has a higher job title and greater status than the man may seem equitable and exciting, because it lifts the burden from the man. However, even if the man can accept these conditions, society cannot. The subsequent blow to his masculinity can cause interpersonal problems if such realities are not anticipated and continually reassessed.

The literature continues to stress that optimal performers are not motivated by "fear of failure," but by a personal set of goals. Optimal performers understand the need for relaxation and the importance of vacations. They are extraordinary delegators and set high standards for their work, but they do not expect perfection.

In summary, the lesson most important to enable managerial women to "have it all" is that each woman must determine what "all" is for her. All women need to understand that choices limit other courses of action and that reaping the benefits also means paying the costs elsewhere. The only way to achieve "it all" is through prioritization, time management, delegation, and the fine art of saying no. Because guilt uses time and emotion unproductively, managerial women must try to avoid or reduce it. Finally, women must recognize that taking care of their own needs is not selfish, but a necessary condition for survival.

CONCLUSION

The most disheartening information revealed in the literature is the insensitivity of male social workers toward women's issues, involving their female staff, colleagues, or clients (Belon & Gould, 1977; Fanshel, 1976; Gould & Kim, 1976; Kravetz and Austin, 1984). Social work agencies and the men who manage them must be made aware that sexism guarantees a waste of human potential, the loss of effective service delivery to their clients, and a loss of income dollars. Until they gain such awareness they may not be motivated to change their traditionally male-oriented policies.

Likewise, female social workers must assert their rights to and expertise in management. By withdrawing from the competition or entering it half-heartedly women will only assure the continuance of male-dominated service systems. Until policies and practices are routinely reviewed for sexist bias and subtle forms of gender discrimination, the inferences drawn from multivariate analyses of positions, salary, and fringe benefits will continue to "blame the victims."

Women who enter management enter with the following cultural and social strikes against them:

1. less cultural acceptance of women as managers—the male model and its attendant stereotypes still prevail
2. stereotypes of women in management, which lead to differential treatment such as discrimination, ostracism, and blaming the victim
3. expectations from both superiors and subordinates that the woman manager is unique among women; women who occupy managerial positions are in no-win situations
4. a socialization process that encourages women and men to relate only as sexual beings, rather than as total beings. Consequently, both parties may bring interactional patterns that are inappropriate to the workplace

5. a socialization process that ascribes to males those qualities associated with competence and power and that ascribes to females those
qualities associated with helpmate and nurturer

Thus, unless examined and corrected, there is a vast array of historical
and traditional beliefs, attitudes, and behaviors that impede the progress of
women in management in human services. This examination and the resultant prescriptions must fall simultaneously on the women aspiring to these
positions and on the organizations. Although public statements and demo-
graphics regarding gender have changed in the recent past and are likely to
continue to change, assumptions supporting the traditional role patterns
have not changed as dramatically.

The first important step is to identify attitudes and behaviors that serve
as barriers within the workplace, without responding to them. At the same
time, one should realize that many women bring feminine traits of sharing,
caring, and support to the workplace, even while adopting some of the male
success methodology. It should prove to be a most happy blend (Levinson,
1978 p. 98).

The vistas for the human services profession are expanding and the
demands for more competent managers are escalating. Meanwhile, the
percentage of men in social work education is decreasing and male membership in the professional association is only approximately 30%. Furthermore,
during the last decade, the percentage of social workers in administrative
roles dropped from 50% in 1969 to 30% in 1985 (Sarri, 1987).

Therefore, the pronouncement for the future is not only that wom-
en should think about applying or be welcomed to apply, but that it is
increasingly essential for the profession that women *plan* for careers in
management. The profession needs more administrators—competent administrators—with a different style and perspective on human service administration. Barriers continue to exist, but none so impenetrable as to
prevent accomplished women from overcoming them. Organizations will
continue to pursue social work managers and women ought to be well-
represented in that pool.

How does it feel to have "put it all together" finally? It may never feel
finished, but it does feel balanced, decisive, and planned. It *is* possible.

Sheila gazes at the conference program and smiles as she sees her name in print
as the keynote speaker at the national conference of "Women Managers in
Human Services." The biography reads impressively, and, satisfied, she leans
back, partially closing her eyes.

The spacious office is indeed a combination of welcoming softness and
business functionality. It is decorated in soft tones, conveying a distinct, but
low-key feminine touch, with couches and a conference table. On her desk rests
a computer and a state-of-the-art telephone.

She allows herself a few minutes of reverie. Could it be that only seven years ago she was uncertain about whether to apply for the associate director's position? How swiftly the two years have passed since she has occupied the office of the executive director.

She glances at the program again and smiles. Both Marsha and Jan are on the program as panelists for the luncheon. How would she ever have advanced without them? Marsha's friendship and encouragement throughout their careers was important for building belief in herself, knowing she was not alone, and being able to share openly the trials and thrills of breaking new ground as a woman manager. Jan's connection and information, her role modeling of a successful, but still feminine manager gave Sheila the impetus to go on several times. She is looking forward to meeting them for dinner at the conference.

That reminds her: she must telephone Deanna, her program director, and encourage her to make the time to attend the conference. Deanna is her protege and Sheila wants to show her off. Additionally, the networking would be important and she wants Deanna to meet Marsha and Jan.

Epilogue

There has been an increasing number of articles and books about the feminist perspective in social work but they have focused primarily on the feminist perspective in a therapeutic rather than a managerial relationship.

Obviously apparent from the previous chapters is the ongoing need to understand more about issues for women in management as well as to attempt to prepare women with the adequate skills, knowledge, and experience to successfully deal with them.

While literature abounds with the concept of mentoring, little empirical research exists, and even less on mentoring in social work. Discussion of career planning and networking are almost nonexistent in the social work literature.

There is a need for increased data bases and research on these and other strategies for individual women and for social service organizations. Sexist attitudes can affect research and publication in these areas. Unfortunately, it has been evident that male administrators and educators have been either oblivious to, or antagonistic to, the essence of differential problems and barriers for women in management in human services.

Until recently, there were very few women in senior academic or executive positions; very few women with doctorates; and not even many women teaching in graduate schools of social work. However, as more women rose to those positions, they were interested in those questions and were also in a position to provide support for junior women who might be interested in those questions.

But when there are women interested in the pursuit of the topics, a next level of problem then becomes clear. There is only a small number of women to serve as research subjects. It presents a potential barrier for comparative statistical analyses. For example, when there are only 20 female deans out of 90, a sample of one-third of those is only 7 female deans. Is this sample "representative" or "atypical?"

Beyond these concerns, the evidence continues to exist that "women's issues" tend to be less valued in academic circles and that editorial biases in journals as well as in promotion and tenure committees preclude the centrality and seminal nature of these kinds of studies for the profession.

For example, there has not been empirical data collected about differential socialization of male and female students to the profession of social work. More importantly, however, is the lack of data relative to institutional barriers that persist in social service agencies such as the absence of parental leave, flex time, or the differential assignment of tasks as they may correlate with the number of women in higher level administrative positions in these agencies.

There appears to be no study of the effect of early and continuous career planning on the career pattern of social workers. This would be a first step before the collection of gender differences can be evaluated on those career patterns. Likewise, the presence or absence of mentors for social workers has not received widespread study. Investigations relative to the presence and the effect of mentors for social workers in management are undocumented. Consequently, there is no useful information for agencies, the professional associations, or social work education for the utility of this strategy for managerial success. Likewise, networking, a strategy more written about in the field of management, is virtually unexamined in the social work literature.

Further exploration of the impact of gender differences on managerial style is clearly useful. Most of the existing literature for this topic was developed in business and industry. The perception of effective management style may clearly be different in social work and social work training might well serve to neutralize gender differences in style.

This book has used literature and research in other fields, as well as social work practice experience, to illustrate issues and sensitize readers. It is hoped that this book has also clearly illustrated the gaps in professional literature and the suggested directions for future research.

References

Austin, C. D., Kravetz, D., & Pollock, K. L. (1985). Experiences of women as social work administrators. *Social Work, 30*(2), 173–179.

Babinec, C. S. (1983). Sex, communication, structures and role specification. *Sociological Focus, 11*(3), 199–210.

Baird, J. E. (1976). Sex differences in group communication: A review of the research. *Quarterly Journal of Speech, 62,* 179–192.

Baird, J. E., & Bradley, P. H. (1979). Styles of management and communication: A comparative study of men and women. *Communication Monographs, 46,* 101–111.

Bakke, L., Edson, S. (1977). Women in management. Moving up? *Social Work, 22,* 512–514.

Bales, R. F., & Slater, P. E. (1955). Role differentiation in small, decision-making groups. In T. Parsons & R. Bales (Eds.), *Family, socialization, and interaction processes* (pp. 259–306). Glencoe, IL: Free Press.

Basil, D. C. (1972). *Women in management.* New York: Dunellen.

Belon, C., & Gould, K. (1977). Not even equals: Sex-related salary inequities. *Social Work, 22*(6) 466–471.

Berkun, C. S. (1984). Women and the field experience: Toward a model of nonsexist field-based learning conditions. *Journal of Education for Social Work, 20*(3), 5–12.

Bolles, R. (1985). *What color is your parachute?* (rev. ed.). Berkeley, CA: Ten Speed Press.

Bradford, D. L., Sargent, A. G., & Sprague, M. S. (1975). The executive man and woman: The issue of sexuality. In F. E. Gordon & M. H. Strober (Eds.). *Bringing women into management* (pp. 39–58). New York: McGraw-Hill.

Brass, D. (1985). Men's and women's networks: A study of interaction patterns and influence in an organization. *Academy of Management Journal, 28,* pp. 327–343.

Buskirk, R. (1980). *Your career: How to plan it, manage it, change it.* Boston, MA: CBI.

Cahill, S. E. (1981). Cross-sex pseudocommunication. *Berkeley Journal of Sociology*, *26*, 75–87.

Calkin, C. L. (1983). *Women administrators: A profile of their advancement*. Paper presented at the annual symposium of the National Association of Social Work, Washington, DC.

Cecil, E. A., Paul, R. J., & Olins, R. A. (1973). Perceived importance of selected variables used to evaluate male and female job applicants. *Personnel Psychology*, *26*(3), 397–404.

Chafetz, J. (1972). Women in social work. *Social Work*, *17*(5), 12–18.

Chafetz, J. (1978). *Masculine, Feminine or Human?* Itasca, IL: F.E. Peacock Publishers.

Chernesky, R. (1980). Women administrators in social work. In E. Norman & A. Mancuso (Eds.), *Women issues and social work practice* (pp. 241–262). Itasca, IL: F.E. Peacock Publishers.

Chernesky, R. (1983). The sex dimension of organizational processes: Its impact on women managers. *Administration in Social Work*, *7*(3/4), 133–143.

Clance, P. (1985). *The imposter phenomenon*. Toronto: Bantam Books.

Clawson, J. & K. Kram (1984). Managing cross-gender mentoring. *Business Horizons*, *27*(3), 22–31.

Collins, B. (1986). Defining feminist social work. *Social Work*, *31*(3), 214–219.

Collins, N. W. (1983). *Professional women and their mentors: A practical guide to mentoring for the woman who wants to get ahead*. Englewood Cliffs, NJ: Prentice-Hall.

Collins, S. (1984). A comparison of top and middle level women administrators in social work, nursing, and education: Career supports and barriers. *Administration in Social Work*, *8*(2), 25–34.

Corcoran, Kevin J., Robbins, S. P., Hepler, S. E., & Magner, G. W. Support systems and scholarly productivity. *Journal of Applied Social Sciences*, *11*(2), 230–242.

Curlee, M. B., & Raymond, F. (1978). The female administrator: Who is she? *Administration in Social Work*, *2*, 307–319.

Dalton, G. W., Thompson, P. H., & Price, R. L. (1977). The four stages of professional careers: A new look at performance by professionals. *Organizational Dynamics*, *6*, 19–42.

Dictionary of Occupational Titles, "Mentoring," U.S. Dept. of Labor Employment and Training Administration, 4th edition, 1977, p. 1370.

Diangson, P., Kravetz, D., & Lipton, J. (1975). Sex role stereotyping and social work education. *Journal of Education for Social Work*, *11*(3), 44–49.

Fanshel, D. (1976). Status differentials: Men and women in social work. *Social Work*, *21*(6), 448–454.

Faver, C. A., Fox, M. F., & Shannon, C. (1983). The educational processes and job equity for the sexes in social work. *Journal of Education for Social Work*, *19*(3), 78–87.

Figler, H. (1979). *The complete job search handbook*. New York: Holt, Rinehart, & Winston.

Finkelstein, C. (1981). Women managers: Career patterns and changes in the United

States. In C. Epstein & R. Coser (Eds.), *Access to power: Cross-national studies of women and elites* (pp. 193–210). London: George Allen, & Unwin.

Fitt, L., & Newton, D. (1981). When the mentor is a man and the protege is a woman. *Harvard Business Review*, 59(2), 56–60.

Forisha, L., & Goldman, B. H. (1981). *Outsiders on the inside: Women and organizations*. Englewood Cliffs, NJ: Prentice-Hall.

Frances, S. J. (1979). Sex differences in nonverbal behavior. *Sex Roles*, 5(4), 519–535.

Friedan, B. (1963). *The feminine mystique*. New York: Norton.

Gerrard, M., Oliver, J. S., & Williams, M. (Eds.). (1976). Women in management. *Proceedings at the conference: Women and men, colleagues in management?* Austin: University of Texas.

Goffman, E. (1966). *Behavior in public places*. New York: Free Press.

Goldberg, S., & Lewis, M. (1969). Play behavior in the year-old infant: Early sex differences. *Child Development*, 40, 21–31.

Hanlan, M. (1977). Women in social work administration: Current role strains. *Administration in Social Work*, (1), 258–267.

Harragan, B. L. (1984). Getting ahead: Management training. *Working Woman*, pp. 380–381.

Haynes, K. (1983). Sexual differences in social work administrators' job satisfaction. *Journal of Social Service Research*, 16(3/4), 57–74.

Haynes, K., & Baute, S. Comparative communication styles between male and female social work administrators. Paper presented at the National Association of Social Workers' Womens Issues Conference, Atlanta, GA. 1986.

Henley, N. (1977). *Body politics: Power, sex, and non-verbal communication*. Englewood Cliffs, NJ: Prentice-Hall.

Hennig, M., & Jardim, A. (1977). *The managerial woman*. New York: Anchor Press/Doubleday.

Horner, M. (1969). Fail! bright women. *Psychology Today*, Vol 3, No. 6, pp. 82–85.

Hyland, M., Curtis, C., & Mason, D. (1985). Fear of success: Motive and cognition. *Journal of Personality and Social Psychology*, 49, 1669–1677.

Imes, S., & Clance, P. (1984). Treatment of the imposter phenomenon in high-achieving women. In C. Brody (Ed.), *Women therapists working with women*, (pp. 69–85).

Jackson, J. M. (1969). The organization and its communications problem. In N. B. Sigband (Ed.), *Communication for management* (pp. 548–556). Glenview, IL: Scott-Foresman.

Jardim, A. (1977). Women executives in the old boys network. *Psychology Today*, 76–81.

Jenkins, M. M. (1980). Toward a model of human leadership. In C. Berryman & V. Eman (Eds.), *Communication, language, and sex* (pp. 149–158). Rowley, MA: Newbury House.

Jennings, P., & Daley, M. (1979). Sex discrimination in social work careers. *Social Work Research and Abstracts*, 15(2), 17–21.

Josefowitz, N. (1980). *Paths to power: A woman's guide from first job to top executive*. Reading, MA: Addison-Wesley.

Kanter, R. M. (1975). Women and the structure of organizations: Explorations of theory and behavior. In M. Millman & R. M. Kanter (Eds.), *Another voice: Feminist perspectives on social life and social science* (pp. 34–74). New York: Anchor Books.

Kanter, R. M. (1977). *Men and women of the corporation*. New York: Basic Books.

Kerson, T. S., & Alexander, L. B. (1979). Strategies for success: Women in social service administration. *Administration in Social Work, 3*(3), 313–327.

Knapman, S. K. (1977). Sex discrimination in family agencies. *Social Work, 22*(6), 461–465.

Kram, K. E. (1983). Phases of the mentor relationship. *Academy of Management, 26*(4), 608–625.

Kram, K. (1985). *Mentoring at Work: Developmental relationships in organizational life*. Glenview, IL: Scott Foresman & Co.

Kravetz, D., & Austin, C. (1984). Women's issues in social service administration: The views and experiences of women administrators. *Administration in Social Work, 8*(4), 25–36.

Kravetz, D. (1976). Sexism in a woman's profession. *Social Work, 21*(6), 421–426.

Kravetz, D., & Jones, L. E. (1982). Career orientations of female social work students: An examination of sex differences. *Journal of Education for Social Work, 18*(3), 77–84.

Kravetz, D. & Austin, C. (1984). Women's Issues in Social Service Administration: The Views and Experiences of Women Administrators. *Administration in Social Work, 8*(4), 25–38.

Kuhn, Elisabeth (1982). "Sex-Related Differences in the Use of Speed Acts as an Indicator of Differences in Communicative Strategies and their Effect on the Hearer." Presentation at the International Sociological Conference, 1982.

Larwood, L., & Wood, M. M. (1977). *Women in management*. Lexington, MA: Lexington Books.

Lee, N. (1980). *Targetting the top: Everything a woman needs to know to develop a successful career in business year after year*. New York: Doubleday & Company.

Levinson, D. J., Darrow, C. N., Klein, E. B., Levinson, M. H., & McKee, B. (1978). *The seasons of a man's life*. New York: Ballantine Books.

Lipman-Blumen, J. (1984). *Gender roles and power*. Englewood Cliffs, NJ: Prentice-Hall.

Machlowitz, M. (1978). *Inside moves: Corporate smarts for women on the way up*. Boulder, CO: Careertrack.

Mai-Dalton, R., & Sullivan, J. (1981). The effects of manager's sex on the assignment to a challenging or a dull task and reasons for the choice. *Academy of Management, 24*(3), 603–612.

McLane, H. J. (1980). *Selecting, developing, and retaining women executives*. New York: Van Nostrand-Reinhold.

Merriam, S. (1983). Mentors and proteges: A critical review of the literature. *Adult Education Quarterly, 33* (3), 161–173.

Mintzberg, H. (1973). *The nature of managerial work*. New York: Harper & Row.

Missirian, A. K. (1982). *The corporate connections: Why executive women need mentors to reach the top*. Englewood Cliffs, NJ: Prentice-Hall.

Molloy, J. T. (1977). *The woman's dress for success book*. New York: Warner Books.

Noe, R. A. (1988). Women and mentoring: A review and research agenda. *Academy of Management Review*, *13*(1), 65–78.

Riley, S., & Wrench, D. (1985). Mentoring among women lawyers. *Journal of Applied Psychology*, *15*, 374–386.

Rosen, B., & Jerdee, T. H. (1974). Sex stereotyping in the executive suite. *Harvard Business Review*, pp. 45–58.

Rosen, B., & Jerdee, T. H. (1978). Perceived sex differences in managerially relevant characteristics. *Sex Roles*, *4*(6), 837–843.

Rubin, A. (1982). Re-examining the impact of sex on salary: The limits of statistical significance. *Social Work Research and Abstracts*, *18*, 24–27.

Sarri, R. (1987). Administration in social welfare. *Encyclopedia of Social Work* (18th ed.) (Vol. 1, pp. 27–40). Silver Spring, MD: National Association of Social Work.

Schein, V. E. (1973). Relationship between sex role stereotypes and requisite management characteristics. *Journal of Applied Psychology*, *57*, 95–100.

Scotch, C. B. (1971). Sex status in social work: Grist for women's liberation. *Social Work*, *16*(3), 5–11.

Shaevitz, M. H. (1984). *The superwoman syndrome*. New York: Warner Books.

Shann, M. H. (1983). Career plans of men and women in gender-dominant professions. *Journal of Vocational Behavior*, *22*(3), 343–356.

Smith, L. (1983). Telegraph, telephone, telewoman. *The Executive Female*, pp. 52–58.

Smith, E., & Grenier, M. (1982). Sources of organizational power for overcoming structural obstacles. *Sex Roles*, *8*, 733–746.

Srinika, T., & Chess, W. A. (1983). Job satisfaction and turnover among social work administrators: A national survey. *Administration in Social Work*, *7*(2), 11–22.

Stafford, B. (1987). The effect of the mentor relationship on graduate social work students. Master's thesis, University of Houston.

Stern, B. B. (1981). *Is networking for you? A working woman's alternative to the old boy system*. Englewood Cliffs, NJ: Prentice-Hall.

Stewart, L. P. and Gudykunst, W. B. (1982). Differential factors influencing the hierarchical level and number of promotions of males and females within an organization. *Academy of Management Journal*, *25*, 586–597.

Summer, R. (1969). *Personal space*. Englewood Cliffs, NJ: Prentice-Hall.

Sutton, J. A. (1982). Sex discrimination among social workers. *Social Work*, *27*(3), 211–217.

Szakacs, J. (1977). Survey indicates social work women losing ground in leadership. *NASW News*, *22*(4), 12.

Taibbi, R. (1983). Supervisors as mentors. *Social Work*, *28*(3), 237–238.

Talbott, J. A., & Bachrach, L. L. (1985). Administrative psychiatry: What sort of job is this for women? *Administration in Mental Health*, *12*(4), 252–263.

Tickamyer, A. R. and Bokemeier, J. L. (1984). Career mobility and satisfaction of women administrators in postsecondary education: A review and research agenda. *Sociological Spectrum*, *4*(2–3), 335–360.

Treasmar, D. (1974). Fear of success: Popular but unproven. *Psychology Today*, pp. 82–85.

Valentich, M., & Gripton, J. (1978). Sexism and sex differences in career management of social workers. *Social Science Journal, 15*(2), 101–111.

Welch, M. S. (1980). *Networking: The great new way for women to get ahead.* New York: Harcourt, Brace, & Jovanovich.

Williams, M., Ho, L., & Fielder, L. (1974). Career patterns: More grist for women's liberation. *Social Work, 19*(4), 463–466.

Witkin-Lanoil, G. (1984). *The female stress syndrome: How to recognize and live with it.* New York: Newmarket Press.

Wong, P. T., Kettlewell, G., & Sproule, C. (1985). On the importance of being masculine: Sex role attribution and women's career advancement. *Sex Roles, 12*, 757–769.

Yamatani, H. (1982). Gender and salary inequity: Statistical interaction effects. *Social Work Research and Abstracts, 18*, 24–27.

York, R. O., Henley, H. C., & Gamble, D. N. (1985). Barriers to the advancement of women in social work administration. *Journal of Social Service Research, 9*(1), 1–15.

York, R., Henley, H. C., & Gamble, D. N. (1987). Sexual discrimination in social work: Is it salary or advancement? *Social Work, 32*(4), 336–339.

York, R., Henley, H., & Gamble, D. (1988). The power of positive mentors: variables associated with women's interest in social work administration. *Journal of Social Work Education, 24*(3), 242–250.

Index